W9-CRQ-562

triumphlearning™
Common Core Coach
Mathematics 6

Dr. Jerry Kaplan
Senior Mathematics Consultant

Common Core Coach, Mathematics, First Edition, Grade 6   T117NA   ISBN-13: 978-1-61997-439-5
Contributing Writer: Ann Petroni McMullen   **Cover Design:** Q2A/Bill Smith   **Cover Illustration:** Stephanie Dalton

Triumph Learning® 136 Madison Avenue, 7th Floor, New York, NY 10016 © 2013 Triumph Learning, LLC. Buckle Down and Coach are imprints of Triumph Learning. All rights reserved. No part of this publication may be reproduced in whole or in part, stored in a retrieval system, or transmitted in any form or by any means, electronic, mechanical, photocopying, recording or otherwise, without written permission from the publisher.

Printed in the United States of America.   10 9 8 7 6 5 4 3 2 1

The National Governors Association Center for Best Practices and Council of Chief State School Officers are the sole owners and developers of the Common Core State Standards, © Copyright 2010. All rights reserved.

Contents

 Problem Solving   Fluency Lesson   Performance Task

Grade 5 | Grade 6 | Grade 7

Grade 5 MD
Convert like measurement units within a given measurement system.

Grade 5 NBT
Understand the place value system.

Perform operations with multi-digit whole numbers and with decimals to hundredths.

Grade 5 NF
Apply and extend previous understandings of multiplication and division to multiply and divide fractions.

Grade 5 G
Graph points on the coordinate plane to solve real-world and mathematical problems.

Grade 6 RP
Understand ratio concepts and use ratio reasoning to solve problems.

Grade 7 RP
Analyze proportional relationships and use them to solve real-world and mathematical problems.

Grade 7 SP
Use random sampling to draw inferences about a population.

Draw informal comparative inferences about two populations.

Investigate chance processes and develop, use, and evaluate probability models.

Domain 1
Ratios and Proportional Relationships

Understanding Ratios

UNDERSTAND A **ratio** can compare a part to a part, a part to the whole, or the whole to a part. The word "to" compares the two terms in a ratio. You can write a ratio in different ways.

Write the ratio of squares to all shapes in three different ways.

Write the ratio in words.

Count the number of squares.

There are 3 squares.

Count the total number of shapes. There are 8 shapes in all.

Write the ratio using the word "to."

▶ The ratio of squares to all shapes is "three to eight."

Write the ratio using a symbol.

A colon (:) is a symbol used to write a ratio.

▶ The ratio of squares to all shapes is 3:8.

Write the ratio using a fraction.

$\frac{3}{8}$ ← Write the first term in the numerator.
← Write the quantity of all terms in the denominator.

▶ The ratio of squares to all shapes is $\frac{3}{8}$.

⟵ Connect

For every fish Nate caught fishing from the shore, Brian caught four fish from his boat in the lake. Write a ratio to represent the situation. Then draw a picture to represent the situation.

1 The situation compares two quantities. It compares the number of fish that Nate caught to the number of fish that Brian caught.

The situation represents a ratio.

2 Write a ratio for the situation.

For every fish Nate caught, Brian caught four fish.

This is the same as saying that Nate caught 1 fish for every 4 fish Brian caught.

▶ The ratio of the number of fish Nate caught to the number of fish Brian caught is 1 to 4, 1:4, or $\frac{1}{4}$.

3 Draw a picture to represent the situation.

Nate caught 1 fish for every 4 fish Brian caught.

Draw 1 fish for Nate and 4 fish for Brian.

▶

    Nate   Brian

MODEL

For every two white roses in a bouquet, the florist uses three red roses. Draw a picture to represent the situation.

Practice

Use the figures below to write each ratio three ways.

1. green to white figures

   _____

2. circles to stars

   _____

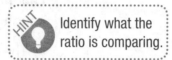

HINT Identify what the ratio is comparing.

3. green figures to total figures

   _____

4. green stars to white stars

   _____

5. white circles to white figures

   _____

6. green circles to green stars

   _____

Use the following address to write each ratio three ways.

36541 Riverside Road

7. numbers to letters

   _____

8. vowels to consonants

   _____

9. consonants to numbers

   _____

10. letters to complete address

    _____

11. complete address to numbers

    _____

12. vowels to letters

    _____

REMEMBER The order is important in a ratio.

Make a drawing to show each ratio. Then write the ratio three ways.

13. The ratio of books to mystery books on a shelf is nine to two.

    _____

14. The ratio of adults to children at the park is three to ten.

    _____

15. The ratio of paws to tails on a tiger is four to one.

    _____

Write a real-world context for each ratio.

16. five to three

_____

_____

17. 2 to 7

_____

_____

18. 4:12

_____

_____

19. $\frac{6}{1}$

_____

_____

Solve.

20. Out of 28 students in the class, 21 wore sneakers to school. What is the ratio of students who wore sneakers to those who did not wear sneakers?

_____

21. Of the 18 students at a dance camp, 6 are boys. What is the ratio of girls to students at the camp?

_____

22. ANALYZE The ratio of games the Falcons won to the games they lost is 7:5. What is the ratio of games won to the total number of games played? Explain.

_____

_____

_____

23. WRITE MATH Write three different ratios for the following situation. Explain what the ratios compare.

Kendra has 2 cats and 3 dogs.

_____

_____

_____

2 Understanding Unit Rates

UNDERSTAND A **rate** is a ratio that compares two quantities with different units of measure. A **unit rate** is a rate in which the second measurement or amount is 1 unit.

Three full vans, all with the same number of seats, hold a total of 36 people. The unit rate is the number of people per 1 van. What is the unit rate?

1 To find the unit rate, find the number of people needed to fill one van. Use drawings to find the unit rate. Draw 3 boxes to represent the 3 vans.

2 Draw bars in each box to represent the people.
Draw one bar in each box to represent one person per van.

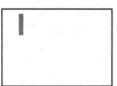 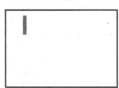 

3 Draw another bar in each box. Then continue to draw one bar in each box until you have drawn 36 bars.

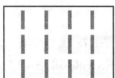  

4 Count the number of bars in each box to find the unit rate.
Each box has 12 bars.

▶ The unit rate is $\frac{12 \text{ people}}{1 \text{ van}}$, or 12 people per van.

← Connect

Three full vans hold 36 people. The number of people per van is the unit rate. What is the number of people per van?

1

Write a ratio to compare the number of people to the number of vans.

number of people : number of vans

36:3

2

Write the ratio in fraction form.

$$\frac{\text{people}}{\text{vans}} \rightarrow \frac{36}{3}$$

3

Write the fraction as division.

The fraction bar means division.

Divide the numerator by the denominator.

$36 \div 3$

4

Divide.

$36 \div 3 = 12$

5

Write the unit rate.

$$\frac{36}{3} = \frac{12}{1}$$

▶ The unit rate is $\frac{12 \text{ people}}{1 \text{ van}}$, or 12 people per van.

DISCUSS

How could you find the unit rate if 4 full vans hold 36 people?

EXAMPLE A A recipe calls for 24 eggs to 4 cups of milk. The unit rate is the number of eggs per cup of milk. What is the number of eggs per cup of milk? How many eggs are needed if 2 cups of milk are used?

1

Write a ratio to compare the number of eggs to the number of cups of milk.

Write the ratio in fraction form.

$$\frac{\text{eggs}}{\text{cups of milk}} \begin{array}{c} \rightarrow \\ \rightarrow \end{array} \frac{24}{4}$$

2

Write the fraction as division.

Divide the numerator by the denominator.

$24 \div 4$

3

Divide.

$24 \div 4 = 6$

4

Write the unit rate.

$$\frac{24}{4} = \frac{6}{1}$$

▶ The unit rate is $\frac{6 \text{ eggs}}{1 \text{ cup milk}}$ or 6 eggs per 1 cup of milk.

5

Use the unit rate to find the number of eggs needed for 2 cups of milk.

Multiply to find the rate for 2 cups of milk.

$$\frac{6 \text{ eggs}}{1 \text{ cup milk}} \times \frac{2}{2} = \frac{12 \text{ eggs}}{2 \text{ cups milk}}$$

▶ 12 eggs are needed if 2 cups of milk are used.

 TRY

A recipe has a ratio of 3 cups of milk to 12 eggs. How many eggs are needed if 12 cups of milk are used?

EXAMPLE B A recipe for one loaf of bread calls for $\frac{3}{4}$ cup of white flour for each cup of whole wheat flour. Rose wants to make 4 loaves of bread. How much whole wheat flour will she need? How much white flour will she need?

1

Identify the unit rate.

The unit rate is $\frac{3}{4}$ cup of white flour per 1 cup of whole wheat flour, $\frac{3}{4}$ to 1, or $\frac{3}{4}$:1.

2

Think about the information you need.

The recipe for one loaf of bread calls for 1 cup of whole wheat flour. Rose wants to make 4 loaves of bread. So, she must multiply each ingredient by 4 to find how much flour she will need.

3

Multiply to find the amount of whole wheat flour Rose will need.

The recipe calls for 1 cup of whole wheat flour.

$1 \times 4 = 4$

▶ Rose will need 4 cups of whole wheat flour to make 4 loaves of bread.

4

Multiply to find the amount of white flour Rose will need.

The recipe calls for $\frac{3}{4}$ cup of white flour.
$\frac{3}{4} \times 4 = \frac{3 \times 4}{4} = \frac{12}{4} = 3$

▶ Rose will need 3 cups of white flour to make 4 loaves of bread.

MODEL

In a recipe for punch, $\frac{1}{4}$ cup of pineapple juice is used for each cup of orange juice. Draw a diagram to model how many cups of pineapple juice are used with 4 cups of orange juice.

Practice

Write a ratio for each rate. Then find the unit rate.

1. 120 miles in 5 hours

   _____

 HINT Use the second term of the ratio to find the unit rate.

2. 96 words in 3 minutes

   _____

3. 208 people in 4 buses

   _____

4. 136 points in 8 games

   _____

5. $2.70 for 3 goldfish

   _____

6. $14 for 7 comic books

   _____

Find each unit rate.

7. 48 grams of protein in 4 servings

   _____

   REMEMBER The second term of a unit rate is always 1.

8. 1,068 miles in 3 hours

   _____

9. 140 students to 5 teachers

   _____

10. $3.60 for 12 eggs

    _____

11. 72 strikeouts in 12 games

    _____

12. 190 feet in 5 seconds

    _____

13. 32 students to 4 parents

    _____

14. 640 miles per 20 gallons

    _____

Find each unit rate. Then write which is the better buy.

15. $0.90 for 2 pens or $1.75 for 5 pens

_____

16. $2.25 for 3 tennis balls or $6.24 for 8 tennis balls

_____

17. $1.92 for 4 apples or $4.20 for 10 apples

_____

18. $24 for 6 pounds of cereal or $45 for 9 pounds of cereal

_____

Choose the best answer.

19. A chef uses 1 cup of cheese per 2 cups of milk in a casserole. How many cups of cheese are needed if the chef uses 6 cups of milk?

A. 2 cups   **B.** 3 cups

C. 5 cups   **D.** 6 cups

20. Javier scored 30 goals in 15 soccer games. Using the unit rate, how many goals will he score in 20 games?

A. 35 goals   **B.** 40 goals

C. 45 goals   **D.** 60 goals

Solve.

21. The coach pays $72 for 18 hamburgers. What is the cost per hamburger?

_____

22. Ayesha's puppy gained 36 pounds in 9 weeks. Using the unit rate, how many pounds did the puppy gain in 5 weeks?

_____

23. (ANALYSIS) Compare and contrast rates and ratios.

_____

_____

_____

3 Using Tables of Equivalent Ratios

A table can be used to show the relationship between two quantities. You can use **equivalent ratios** to find a missing value in a table.

EXAMPLE A The table shows the relationship between the number of green beads and the number of blue beads Mindy uses when she makes bracelets.

Green Beads	2	4	6	8	10
Blue Beads	5	10	15	20	?

How many blue beads does Mindy use when she uses 10 green beads?

1

Write the first two ratios as fractions.

First ratio: $\dfrac{\text{green beads}}{\text{blue beads}} = \dfrac{2}{5}$ Second ratio: $\dfrac{\text{green beads}}{\text{blue beads}} = \dfrac{4}{10}$

2

Look for a pattern to see how the first ratio can be changed to the second, third, and fourth ratios.

$$\frac{2}{5} = \frac{2 \times 2}{5 \times 2} = \frac{4}{10} \qquad \frac{2}{5} = \frac{2 \times 3}{5 \times 3} = \frac{6}{15} \qquad \frac{2}{5} = \frac{2 \times 4}{5 \times 4} = \frac{8}{20}$$

The ratios are equivalent.

3

Extend the pattern to find the fifth ratio.

Multiply each term in the first ratio by 5.
$$\frac{2}{5} = \frac{2 \times 5}{5 \times 5} = \frac{10}{25}$$

$$\frac{\text{green beads}}{\text{blue beads}} = \frac{10}{25}$$

▶ Mindy uses 25 blue beads when she uses 10 green beads.

DISCUSS

Explain how to find the number of green beads Mindy uses when she uses 35 blue beads.

EXAMPLE B The table shows the relationship between the number of dog collars Travis can make and the number of hours he takes to make the collars.

Number of Hours	3	9	15	24
Number of Dog Collars	8	?	?	?

Use ratios to complete the table.

1

Decide what ratio the table shows.

The table shows the ratio of hours to dog collars, or $\frac{\text{hours}}{\text{dog collars}}$.

2

Write equivalent ratios for the first ratio and the other ratios in the table.

Compare the numerators of the equivalent ratios to decide how the terms are changing in each ratio.

$\frac{3}{8} = \frac{9}{?}$ Think: $3 \times \mathbf{3} = 9$ So $\frac{3}{8} = \frac{9}{24}$
$8 \times \mathbf{3} = 24$

$\frac{3}{8} = \frac{15}{?}$ Think: $3 \times \mathbf{5} = 15$ So $\frac{3}{8} = \frac{15}{40}$
$8 \times \mathbf{5} = 40$

$\frac{3}{8} = \frac{24}{?}$ Think: $3 \times \mathbf{8} = 24$ So $\frac{3}{8} = \frac{24}{64}$
$8 \times \mathbf{8} = 64$

3

Use the equivalent ratios to complete the table.

Number of Hours	3	9	15	24
Number of Dog Collars	8	24	40	64

CHECK

How many dog collars can Travis make in 21 hours?

EXAMPLE C The table shows the relationship between the total number of games and the total number of weeks the games were played.

Number of Games	2	4	6	8	10
Number of Weeks	?	?	?	4	?

Complete the table. Then list the ratios as **ordered pairs**.

1 Decide what ratio the table shows and which ratio is known.

The table shows the ratio of games to weeks, or $\frac{\text{games}}{\text{weeks}}$.

From the table, 8 games were played in week 4. The ratio is $\frac{8}{4}$.

2 Use the known ratio to find the first ratio in the table.

As one term in a ratio changes due to multiplication or division, the other unit changes in the same way.

$\frac{8}{4} = \frac{2}{?}$ Think: $8 \div 4 = 2$, so divide the denominator by 4.

$\frac{8}{4} = \frac{8 \div 4}{4 \div 4} = \frac{2}{1}$

3 Use the first ratio to find the remaining ratios.

$\frac{2}{1} = \frac{4}{?}$ Think: $2 \times 2 = 4$, so multiply the denominator by 2. $\frac{2}{1} = \frac{2 \times 2}{1 \times 2} = \frac{4}{2}$

$\frac{2}{1} = \frac{6}{?}$ Think: $2 \times 3 = 6$, so multiply the denominator by 3. $\frac{2}{1} = \frac{2 \times 3}{1 \times 3} = \frac{6}{3}$

$\frac{2}{1} = \frac{10}{?}$ Think: $2 \times 5 = 10$, so multiply the denominator by 5. $\frac{2}{1} = \frac{2 \times 5}{1 \times 5} = \frac{10}{5}$

4 Use the equivalent ratios to complete the table.

▶
Number of Games	2	4	6	8	10
Number of Weeks	1	2	3	4	5

5 List the ratios as ordered pairs.

An ordered pair is shown as (x, y).

The first coordinate, or the **x-coordinate**, is the number of games.

The second coordinate, or the **y-coordinate**, is the number of weeks.

▶ The ordered pairs are (2, 1), (4, 2), (6, 3), (8, 4), and (10, 5).

TRY

Write the ordered pair for the number of weeks needed to play 16 games.

EXAMPLE D Use the ordered pairs from Example C. Plot the ordered pairs on a **coordinate plane**.

1

Decide what each axis represents on the coordinate plane.

The horizontal axis is called the **x-axis**. It shows the location of the x-coordinate. In these ordered pairs, the x-coordinate represents the number of games.

The vertical axis is called the **y-axis**. It shows the location of the y-coordinate. In these ordered pairs, the y-coordinate is the number of weeks.

2

List the ordered pairs.

(2, 1), (4, 2), (6, 3), (8, 4), (10, 5)

3

Label the axes. Plot the first ordered pair.

The first ordered pair is (2, 1).

Start at the **origin**. Move 2 units to the right. Then move up 1 unit. Plot the point.

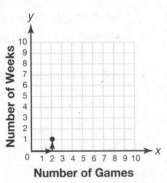

4

Plot the remaining ordered pairs.

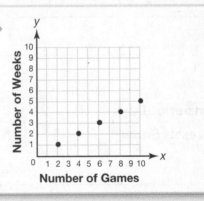

DISCUSS

Explain how you plotted the remaining ordered pairs.

Practice

For questions 1–3, use equivalent ratios to complete each table.

1.

Number of Hours	3	6	9	12	15
Number of Miles	20	40	60	?	?

2.

Number of Teachers	4	12	16	24	32
Number of Students	12	?	?	?	?

> **HINT** As one unit in a ratio changes, the other unit changes in the same way.

3.

Number of Words	25	75	125	150	200
Number of Minutes	?	?	?	6	?

For questions 4 and 5, use equivalent ratios to complete each table. List the ratios in each table as ordered pairs. Then plot the ordered pairs on the coordinate plane.

4.

x	10	20	40	50	80
y	1				

_____

_____

_____

_____

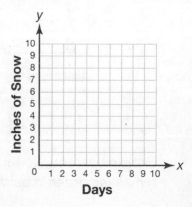

> **REMEMBER** To plot an ordered pair (x, y), start at the origin. Move horizontally x units and then vertically y units.

5.

Number of Days	1	2	3	4	5
Inches of Snow			6		

_____

_____

_____

_____

For questions 6 and 7, use the information given to complete the tables.

6. A recipe uses 2 cups of cooked rice and 3 cups of milk. Create a table of equivalent ratios that shows the relationship between the number of cups of rice and the number of cups of milk used for the recipe.

Cups of Rice					
Cups of Milk					

7. For every 15 sit-ups Ryan does, he does 10 push-ups. Create a table of equivalent ratios that shows the relationship between the number of sit-ups and the number of push-ups Ryan does.

Number of Sit-ups					
Number of Push-ups					

Complete the table and graph.

8. Every 3 days, students in a fitness class run 2 miles. Use equivalent ratios to complete the table. Plot the corresponding ordered pairs on the coordinate plane.

Number of Days	Number of Miles
3	
6	
9	

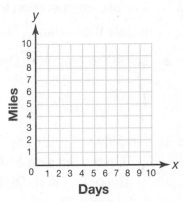

Solve.

9. (REASON) Which of the following ratios is **not** equivalent to the ratio $\frac{5}{6}$? Explain.
$\frac{10}{12}, \frac{13}{14}, \frac{15}{18}, \frac{25}{30}$

_____

_____

_____

10. (STRUCTURE) Explain how you completed the table of equivalent ratios in question 7.

_____

_____

_____

Problem Solving: Unit Rates

Felicia's Ride

READ

Felicia takes 4 hours to ride her bike 56 miles. She rides at a constant speed during the 4-hour ride. What is her **unit rate** in miles per hour?

PLAN

Write an equation to represent the problem.
The number of miles per hour Felicia rides is her unit rate.
Let m = the number of miles Felicia rides per hour.
The number of hours Felicia rides multiplied by her unit rate is equal to the distance she rides.

$4 \times m = 56$

SOLVE

Step 1: Choose an operation to solve the equation. Use the opposite operation to isolate the variable. The opposite of multiplication is _____.

Step 2: Solve the equation. Divide both sides by 4.

$$4 \times m = 56$$
$$\frac{4 \times m}{4} = \frac{56}{4}$$

Step 3: Simplify.
On the left side of the equation, $4 \div 4 = 1$, so the 4s cancel, leaving $1m$ or m. On the right side of the equation, compute $56 \div 4$.

$$\frac{\cancel{4} \times m}{\cancel{4}} = \frac{56}{4}$$
$$m = \underline{\hspace{1cm}}$$

CHECK

Substitute the value found for m in the original equation.

$$4 \times m = 56$$

$4 \times$ _____ $\overset{?}{=} 56$

_____ = _____

▶ Felicia's unit rate is _____ miles per hour.

Tennis Camp

READ

There are 3 instructors per 18 students at a tennis camp. At that rate, how many instructors are needed for 30 students?

PLAN

First find the unit rate of students to instructors. Then use the unit rate to find the number of instructors needed for 30 students.

SOLVE

Step 1: Find the unit rate.

Write the ratio of students to instructors: $\dfrac{\text{students}}{\text{instructors}} = \dfrac{\Box}{\Box}$

Divide to find the unit rate: $18 \div 3 =$ _____

The unit rate is _____ students per instructor.

Step 2: Write an equation using the unit rate.

Let $n =$ the number of instructors needed for 30 students.
The number of students divided by the number of students per instructor is equal to the number of instructors needed.

$30 \div \Box = n$

Step 3: Simplify the equation.

$n =$ _____

CHECK

Use a tape diagram to check the relationship between the number of instructors and the number of students.

instructors	1	2	3	4	5
students	6	12	18	24	30

The tape diagram supports the relationship. It shows that the number of students is always 6 times the number of instructors.

There is 1 instructor for 6 students, 2 instructors for 12 students, 3 instructors for 18 students, _____ instructors for 24 students, and _____ instructors for 30 students.

▶ So _____ instructors are needed for 30 students.

The Farmer's Market

READ

At the farmer's market, 8 apples cost $5.20. If each apple costs the same amount, what is the price per apple?

PLAN

Write an equation to represent the problem.

The price per apple is the unit cost.

The number of apples times the cost per apple is equal to the total cost.

Let p = the price per apple.

$8 \times p = \$5.20$

Find the unit cost.

SOLVE

Find the unit cost.

Write a ratio of cost to number of apples: $\dfrac{5.20}{8}$

Simplify to find the unit cost: $\dfrac{5.20}{8} = \dfrac{5.20 \div \square}{8 \div \square} = \dfrac{\square}{1}$

So the unit cost is _____.

CHECK

Substitute the unit rate for p in the original equation.

$\qquad 8 \times p = 5.20$

$8 \times$ _____ $\overset{?}{=} 5.20$

$\qquad$ _____ $=$ _____

▶ The price per apple is _____.

Art Supply Order

READ

An order of 5 paintbrushes costs $3.50. If each paintbrush costs the same amount, what is the unit cost? What is the cost for an order of 3 paintbrushes?

PLAN

First, find the unit cost of 1 paintbrush.

Let c = the cost of one paintbrush.

$$\frac{\$3.50}{5} = \frac{c}{1}$$

Then use the unit cost to find the total cost of 3 paintbrushes.

SOLVE

Find the unit cost, c.

$$\frac{3.50}{5} = \frac{3.50 \div \boxed{}}{5 \div \boxed{}} = \frac{\boxed{}}{1}$$

$c =$ _____

Find the total cost of 3 paintbrushes.

$3 \times$ _____ = _____

CHECK

Use a double number line to check the relationship between the number of paintbrushes and the total cost.

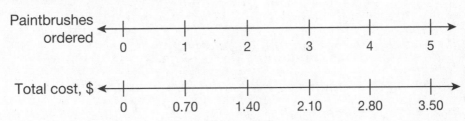

The double number line supports the relationship. It shows that the total cost is always $0.70 times the number of paintbrushes ordered.

▶ The unit cost of a paintbrush is _____. An order of 3 paintbrushes costs _____.

Practice

Use the 4-step problem-solving process to solve each problem.

1. **READ** It takes Karl 6 hours to drive 372 miles. If he drives at a constant speed during the 6 hours, what is his unit rate? At this rate, how far will Karl drive in 8 hours?

   PLAN _____

   _____

   SOLVE

   CHECK

2. Harper bought 4 chairs for $232. What is the unit price? How much will 6 chairs cost?

3. A painter uses 2 tubes of black paint for every 6 tubes of white paint to paint a mural. At that rate, how many tubes of black paint are used if 15 tubes of white paint are used?

4. At Bob's Binders, a set of 3 notebooks costs $4.20. At Pam's Paper Place, a set of 4 notebooks costs $5.20. What is the unit price of the notebooks at each store? Which is the better buy?

5. Ms. Compra bought 5 markers for $4.75. At this price, how much will 4 markers cost? How much will 10 markers cost?

5 Using Percent

EXAMPLE A At the book fair, 40% of the books sold were science related. For every 100 books sold, how many were science related?

1

Use a model to show 40%.

A **percent** is a special ratio. It is a rate per 100.

A 10 by 10 grid has 100 equal parts.

40% means 40 out of 100 equal parts.

Shade 40 parts to show 40%.

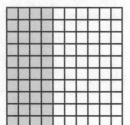

2

Write an equivalent ratio to show the percent.

40% is equivalent to 40 per 100 or $\frac{40}{100}$.

3

Use the ratio to find the number of science-related books sold per 100.

$40\% = \frac{40}{100}$

40% of $100 = \frac{40}{100} \times 100 = \frac{400}{100} = 40$

40 out of 100 books sold were science related.

▶ For every 100 books sold, 40 were science related.

MODEL

Explain how to use the model to show how many books sold per 100 were not science related. What percent of the books sold were not science related?

EXAMPLE B In a jar of 500 beads, 30% are red. How many of the beads are red?

1

Understand what you have to find.

Find 30% of 500 to find the number of red beads.

2

Write an expression for 30% of 500.

30% of 500 means 30% times 500.

30% of 500 = 30% × 500

3

Write the percent as a ratio.

$30\% = \frac{30}{100}$

4

Simplify the expression.

$30\% \times 500 = \frac{30}{100} \times 500$ ← Substitute the ratio for the percent.

$\qquad\qquad = \frac{30}{100} \times \frac{500}{1}$ ← Write 500 as a fraction.

$\qquad\qquad = \frac{15,000}{100}$ ← Multiply the numerators. Then multiply the denominators.

$\qquad\qquad = 150$ ← Simplify.

5

Use a tape diagram to illustrate the percents.

	10%	20%	30%	40%	50%	60%	70%	80%	90%	100%
50	100	150	200	250	300	350	400	450	500	

red beads

total number of beads

▶ There are 150 red beads in the jar.

DISCUSS

Explain how to use the tape diagram to find 80% of 500.

EXAMPLE C 21 is 70% of what number?

1

Make a tape diagram to model the problem.

If you know the part and the percent, you can find the whole.

	10%	20%	30%	40%	50%	60%	70%	80%	90%	100%
							21			

21 is part of the whole. It is 70% of the whole.

2

Use the tape diagram to find the size of each part.

There are 7 equal parts up to 21.

Think: What number times 7 is equal to 21?

$3 \times 7 = 21$, so each part increases by 3.

Each part is 10% on the tape diagram, so 10% of the whole is 3.

3

Complete the tape diagram.

10% of the whole is 3.

Count by 3s to complete the tape diagram.

	10%	20%	30%	40%	50%	60%	70%	80%	90%	100%
	3	6	9	12	15	18	21	24	27	30

4

Use the tape diagram to find the whole.

100% is the whole. 30 is 100% of the whole.

▶ 21 is 70% of 30.

CHECK

What is 70% of 30? Explain.

Problem Solving

READ

At Shaun's Skate World, 18 of the skateboards in stock are on sale. If 20% of the skateboards in stock are on sale, how many skateboards are in stock?

PLAN

18 is 20% of the skateboards in stock.

Use a tape diagram to model the problem.

Complete the tape diagram to find the number of skateboards in stock.

SOLVE

Make the tape diagram.

10%	20%	30%	40%	50%	60%	70%	80%	90%	100%
	18								

There are _____ equal parts up to 18.

Think: What number times _____ is equal to 18?

$2 \times$ _____ $= 18$, so each part increases by _____.

Each part is 10% on the tape diagram, so 10% of the whole is _____.

Count by _____ to complete the tape diagram.

10%	20%	30%	40%	50%	60%	70%	80%	90%	100%
9	18	27	36	45	54	63	72	81	90

What number is 100% of the tape diagram? _____

CHECK

Look back at the completed tape diagram.

What is 20% of the total? _____

Does the number match the quantity in the problem? _____

▶ There are _____ skateboards in stock at Shaun's Skate World.

Practice

Write a percent for each situation.

1. 20 out of 100 people _____

2. 7 out of 10 stores _____

 HINT Write an equivalent ratio to show the rate per 100.

3. 65 votes for Derek per 100 voters _____

Find the percent of each number.

4. 20% of 20

5. 10% of 30

6. 60% of 400

_____

_____

_____

REMEMBER You can use a tape diagram to model the percent.

7. 80% of 40

8. 50% of 60

9. 30% of 200

_____

_____

_____

10. 70% of 600

11. 40% of 50

12. 90% of 300

_____

_____

_____

Make a tape diagram to find each percent.

13. 5 is 10% of what number? _____

14. 75 is 50% of what number? _____

15. 12 is 30% of what number? _____

16. 48 is 80% of what number? _____

17. 120 is 60% of what number? _____

18. 50 is 20% of what number? _____

Choose the best answer.

19. What is 5% of 200?

    A. 5

    B. 10

    C. 20

    D. 25

20. 72 is 60% of what number?

    A. 12

    B. 112

    C. 120

    D. 172

Solve.

21. A play ran for 100 performances. The theater was full for 85% of the performances. For how many performances was the theater **not** full?

_____

22. In a survey of 800 students, 70% said they liked pop music. How many students surveyed like pop music?

_____

23. In a batch of lightbulbs, 30% are tinted. If 45 lightbulbs are tinted, how many light bulbs are in the batch?

_____

24. Keith spent 60% of his birthday money at the mall. If he spent $24 at the mall, how much money did Keith receive for his birthday?

_____

25. CRITIQUE Taylor says that 40% of 50 is the same amount as 50% of 40. Is Taylor correct? Explain.

_____

_____

_____

26. WRITE MATH Explain how to use a tape diagram to find 90% of 180.

_____

_____

_____

LESSON 6

Using Ratios to Convert Measurement Units

Objects can be measured using either the **customary system** or the **metric system**. We can measure length, **mass**, and **capacity**. We can also convert the measurements within a system.

EXAMPLE A Which is longer, 5 feet or 58 inches?

1

Write the ratio for feet to inches.

You can use ratios to convert measurement units. In a ratio, as one unit changes, the other unit changes in the same way.

Use the measurement equivalence:
1 foot = 12 inches.

$$\frac{\text{feet}}{\text{inches}} = \frac{1}{12}$$

2

Write an equivalent ratio to show the number of inches in 2 feet.

Multiply both terms of the ratio by 2.

$$\frac{1}{12} = \frac{1 \times 2}{12 \times 2} = \frac{2}{24}$$

So 2 ft = 24 in.

3

Continue writing equivalent ratios until the number of inches is 58 or greater.

3 ft = ? in.

Multiply both terms of the ratio by 3.

$$\frac{1}{12} = \frac{1 \times 3}{12 \times 3} = \frac{3}{36}$$

So 3 ft = 36 in.

4 ft = ? in.

Multiply both terms of the ratio by 4.

$$\frac{1}{12} = \frac{1 \times 4}{12 \times 4} = \frac{4}{48}$$

So 4 ft = 48 in.

5 ft = ? in.

Multiply both terms of the ratio by 5.

$$\frac{1}{12} = \frac{1 \times 5}{12 \times 5} = \frac{5}{60}$$

So 5 ft = 60 in.

4

Compare.

5 ft = 60 in.

60 in. > 58 in.

So 5 ft > 58 in.

▶ 5 feet is longer than 58 inches.

DISCUSS

Explain how to use equivalent ratios to find the number of feet in 26 yards.

Use *Math Tool: Tables of Measurement Units*.

EXAMPLE B How many quarts are in 3 gallons?

1

Write the ratio of quarts to gallons.

Use the measurement equivalence:
4 quarts = 1 gallon.

$$\frac{quarts}{gallons} = \frac{4}{1}$$

2

Use a tape diagram to model the ratio.

The tape diagram shows that
4 quarts = 1 gallon.

Quarts	1	2	3	4
Gallons		1		

3

Extend the tape diagram to find the equivalence.

Use the tape diagram to show 3 gallons.

Draw 4 quarts for every gallon.

Quarts	1	2	3	4	5	6	7	8	9	10	11	12
Gallons		1				2				3		

4

Use the tape diagram to record the number of quarts in 3 gallons.

▶ There are 12 quarts in 3 gallons.

TRY

Use a tape diagram to find how many pints are in 3 quarts.

EXAMPLE C Which is longer, 72 centimeters or 7 meters?

1

Write the ratio of centimeters to meters.

Use the measurement equivalence:
100 centimeters = 1 meter.

$$\frac{\text{centimeters}}{\text{meters}} = \frac{100}{1}$$

2

Write an equivalent ratio to find the number of centimeters in 7 meters.

Multiply both terms of the ratio by 7.

$$\frac{100}{1} = \frac{100 \times 7}{1 \times 7} = \frac{700}{7}$$

So 700 cm = 7 m

3

Compare 72 cm and 7 m.

7 m = 700 cm

72 cm < 700 cm

So 72 cm < 7 m

▶ 7 meters is longer than 72 centimeters.

TRY

How many centimeters are in 150 millimeters?

Use *Math Tool: Tables of Measurement Units.*

Relevant Ratios

Use Math Tool: Tables of Measurement Units for this activity.

Work with a partner to complete the tables.

1. Choose six different objects in your classroom. For example, choose the door in your classroom. For the time table, choose an event such as the length of a song. Record the names of the objects and the event in the first empty column in the tables.

2. Estimate the measures of the objects and the event you chose. Record the values in the Estimate column. Do not use the same unit of measure for all the objects.

3. Select units to which you will convert your estimated measures. Record these units in the Conversion Units column. For example, if your estimate was in feet and you are going to convert feet to inches, record "inches" in this column.

4. Determine the ratios you will use to convert your estimated measures. Record these ratios in the Conversion Ratio column.

5. Write the estimates in the converted units in the Conversion column.

Customary Units

	Object	Estimate	Conversion Units	Conversion Ratio	Conversion
Length					
Capacity					
Weight					

Metric Units

	Object	Estimate	Conversion Units	Conversion Ratio	Conversion
Length					
Capacity					
Mass					

Time

Event	Estimate	Conversion Units	Conversion Ratio	Conversion

Practice

Use *Math Tool: Tables of Measurement Units.*

Use ratios to convert each measurement.

1. 24 ft = _____ yd

2. 96 oz = _____ lb

 HINT Check the *Math Tool: Tables of Measurement Units* to make accurate conversions.

3. 4 h = _____ min

4. 20 mm = _____ cm

5. 16 L = _____ mL

6. 9,000 g = _____ kg

7. 36 gal = _____ qt

8. 2 ft = _____ in.

9. 5 km = _____ cm

10. 1.4 kg = _____ g

11. 6 pt = _____ c

12. 120 h = _____ d

Compare. Write >, <, or =.

13. 320 s _____ 4 min

14. 5 yd _____ 175 in.

15. 800 mm _____ 80 cm

REMEMBER You can change yards to feet and then feet to inches.

16. 2 lb _____ 42 oz

17. 6 km _____ 6,100 cm

18. 3 g _____ 450 mg

19. 3 qt _____ 6 pt

20. 35 L _____ 2 kL

21. 20 ft _____ 6 yd

22. 70 cm _____ 7 m

23. 2 gal _____ 15 pt

24. 1 d _____ 38 h

Solve.

25. Which is a longer piece of ribbon, one that is 635 millimeters long or one that is 535 centimeters long? How do you know?

_____

26. Which pitcher has a greater capacity, one that holds 2 gallons or one that holds 12 quarts? How do you know?

_____

27. Which melon has a greater mass, one that is 4 kilograms or one that is 4,100 grams? How do you know?

_____

28. Which class lasts longer, one that is 3 hours long or one that is 175 minutes long? How do you know?

_____

Choose the best answer.

29. Which is the longest?

 A. 2 km

 B. 25 m

 C. 2,500 cm

 D. 3,000 mm

30. Which has the least capacity?

 A. 1 gal

 B. 4 qt

 C. 6 pt

 D. 15 c

Solve.

31. Rylie drinks 2 cups of water from a 1-quart bottle of water. How much water is left in the bottle?

 _____

32. A track is 200 meters long. How many times must Julius run around the track to run 3 kilometers?

 _____

33. REASON How can you use the metric prefixes *milli-*, *centi-*, and *kilo-* to help you decide if a metric conversion is reasonable?

 _____

 _____

 _____

34. CONSTRUCT How many cups equal 2 gallons? Explain how you did the conversion.

 _____

 _____

 _____

1 Review

Use the following information for questions 1–3.

Jeremy's password is the combination of letters and numbers shown below. Use Jeremy's password to write each ratio three ways.

2 7 R Q A 5 8 E 3

1. letters to numbers

_____

2. odd to even numbers

_____

3. vowels to letters

_____

Find each unit rate.

4. 720 kilometers per 15 liters

_____

5. 2,736 yards in 8 seconds

_____

6. $5.85 for 9 rolls

_____

7. 224 hits in 14 games

_____

8. 288 markers in 12 boxes

_____

9. 348 words in 6 minutes

_____

For questions 10 and 11, use equivalent ratios to complete each table.

10.

Number of Hours	6	12	24	36	54
Number of Meters	18				

11.

Number of Pages	80	160	280	320	400
Number of Books				8	

Write a percent for each situation.

12. 75 out of 100 students

_____

13. 3 out of 10 movies

_____

14. 20 votes for Erin per 100 voters

_____

Find the percent of each number.

15. 30% of 80

_____

16. 50% of 30

_____

17. 90% of 500

_____

18. 20% of 600

_____

Use a tape diagram to find each percent.

19. 24 is 40% of what number? _____

20. 56 is 70% of what number? _____

21. 15 is 10% of what number? _____

22. 18 is 60% of what number? _____

Use ratios to convert each measurement. Use *Math Tool: Tables of Measurement Units*.

23. 61 km = _____ m

24. 3 d = _____ h

25. 45 ft = _____ yd

26. 6 gal = _____ qt

27. 200 cm = _____ mm

28. 7,000 mL = _____ L

29. 20 c = _____ qt

30. 5 ft = _____ in.

31. 144 oz = _____ lb

32. Every 2 days, Kareem swims 10 laps. Use ratios to complete the table. Plot the corresponding ordered pairs on the coordinate plane.

Number of Days	Number of Laps
2	
4	
6	
8	

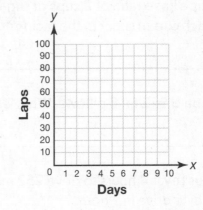

Choose the best answer.

33. Kimberly uses 1 cup of walnuts for every 2 cups of raisins when making trail mix. How many cups of walnuts will she need if she uses 8 cups of raisins?

    A. 3 c

    B. 4 c

    C. 5 c

    D. 6 c

34. A ceramics teacher orders 5 blocks of gray clay for every 3 blocks of red clay. How many blocks of gray clay will the teacher order if she orders 15 blocks of red clay?

    A. 17

    B. 20

    C. 25

    D. 28

35. In a rock collection, 60% of the rocks are quartz. If the collection contains 35 rocks, how many are quartz?

    A. 18

    B. 21

    C. 25

    D. 29

36. The ribbon on a spool is 10 yards long. How many 6-inch pieces of ribbon can be cut from the spool?

    A. 30

    B. 40

    C. 50

    D. 60

Solve.

37. Jesse ran nearly three laps around the track for every lap his grandfather walked. Write the ratio of Jesse's laps around the track to his grandfather's laps.

_____

38. A recipe has a ratio of 2 cups of sugar to 6 cups of flour. How many cups of flour are used for each cup of sugar in the recipe?

_____

39. Uma paid $42 for 6 pillows. What is the unit price? How much would 9 pillows cost?

_____

40. It takes Levar 4 hours to drive 252 miles. What is Levar's unit rate? At this rate, how far will Levar drive in 7 hours?

_____

Oatmeal Ratios

This label shows some nutrition information and a recipe for one serving of oatmeal.

Oatmeal

Serving: $\frac{1}{2}$ cup (40 grams)

Nutrition Information

Total carbohydrate	27 g
Dietary fiber	4 g
Protein	5 g
Calories 150	**From fat** 25

Recipe

Water	1 c
Oats	$\frac{1}{2}$ c

1. How many cups of oats are needed for 8 servings of oatmeal? How do you know?

_____

2. How many cups of oats are needed for 5 servings of oatmeal? How do you know?

_____

3. What is the ratio of total carbohydrate to protein in one serving of oatmeal? Does the ratio change with additional servings of oatmeal? Explain.

_____

_____

4. In oatmeal, 50% of the dietary fiber is soluble fiber. How many grams of the dietary fiber in one serving of oatmeal is soluble fiber? Explain.

_____

_____

5. What percent of one serving of oatmeal is made up of dietary fiber? Explain.

_____

_____

Grade 5 | Grade 6 | Grade 7

Grade 5 NBT

Understand the place value system.

Perform operations with multi-digit whole numbers and with decimals to hundredths.

Grade 5 NF

Use equivalent fractions as a strategy to add and subtract fractions.

Apply and extend previous understandings of multiplication and division to multiply and divide fractions.

Grade 5 G

Graph points on the coordinate plane to solve real-world and mathematical problems.

Grade 6 NS

Apply and extend previous understandings of multiplication and division to divide fractions by fractions.

Compute fluently with multi-digit numbers and find common factors and multiples.

Apply and extend previous understandings of numbers to the system of rational numbers.

Grade 7 RP

Analyze proportional relationships and use them to solve real-world and mathematical problems.

Grade 7 NS

Apply and extend previous understandings of operations with fractions to add, subtract, multiply, and divide rational numbers.

Grade 7 EE

Use properties of operations to generate equivalent expressions.

Solve real-life and mathematical problems using numerical and algebraic expressions and equations.

Grade 7 G

Draw, construct, and describe geometrical figures and describe the relationships between them.

Solve real-life and mathematical problems involving angle measure, area, surface area, and volume.

Domain 2
The Number System

Interpreting and Computing Quotients of Fractions

UNDERSTAND Use models to help divide fractions.

Divide $\frac{3}{4} \div \frac{3}{8}$ means find how many groups of $\frac{3}{8}$ are in $\frac{3}{4}$.

1

Use models to show $\frac{3}{4}$.

| $\frac{1}{4}$ | $\frac{1}{4}$ | $\frac{1}{4}$ | |

2

Place $\frac{1}{8}$ models under the models for $\frac{3}{4}$.

| $\frac{1}{4}$ | $\frac{1}{4}$ | $\frac{1}{4}$ |
| $\frac{1}{8}$ $\frac{1}{8}$ | $\frac{1}{8}$ $\frac{1}{8}$ | $\frac{1}{8}$ $\frac{1}{8}$ |

3

Separate the $\frac{1}{8}$ models into groups of $\frac{3}{8}$.

| $\frac{1}{4}$ | $\frac{1}{4}$ | $\frac{1}{4}$ |
| $\frac{1}{8}$ $\frac{1}{8}$ | $\frac{1}{8}$ $\frac{1}{8}$ | $\frac{1}{8}$ $\frac{1}{8}$ |

$\frac{3}{8}$ $\frac{3}{8}$

4

There are 2 groups of $\frac{3}{8}$ in $\frac{3}{4}$.

▶ $\frac{3}{4} \div \frac{3}{8} = 2$

←⊏ Connect

Divide. $\frac{3}{4} \div \frac{3}{8}$

1

To divide fractions, first write the **reciprocal** of the **divisor**.

The divisor is $\frac{3}{8}$.

Its reciprocal is $\frac{8}{3}$.

2

Write the division problem as a multiplication problem. Multiply the **dividend** by the reciprocal of the divisor.

$$\frac{3}{4} \div \frac{3}{8} = \frac{3}{4} \times \frac{8}{3}$$

3

Multiply the fractions.

Multiply the numerators. Then multiply the denominators.

$$\frac{3}{4} \div \frac{3}{8} = \frac{3}{4} \times \frac{8}{3} = \frac{3 \times 8}{4 \times 3} = \frac{24}{12}$$

4

Write the product in simplest form.

$$\frac{24}{12} = 2$$

▶ $\frac{3}{4} \div \frac{3}{8} = 2$

Use multiplication to check your answer.

$2 \times \frac{3}{8} =$ _____

EXAMPLE Divide. $\frac{8}{10} \div \frac{1}{5}$

1

Write the division problem as a multiplication problem. Multiply the dividend by the reciprocal of the divisor.

$$\frac{8}{10} \div \frac{1}{5} = \frac{8}{10} \times \frac{5}{1}$$

2

Multiply the fractions.

$$\frac{8}{10} \times \frac{5}{1} = \frac{8 \times 5}{10 \times 1} = \frac{40}{10}$$

3

Write the product in simplest form.

$$\frac{40}{10} = 4$$

4

Use models to justify the answer.

$\frac{1}{10}$	$\frac{1}{10}$	$\frac{1}{10}$	$\frac{1}{10}$	$\frac{1}{10}$	$\frac{1}{10}$	$\frac{1}{10}$	$\frac{1}{10}$

$\frac{1}{5}$	$\frac{1}{5}$	$\frac{1}{5}$	$\frac{1}{5}$

There are 4 groups of $\frac{1}{5}$ in $\frac{8}{10}$.

▶ $\frac{8}{10} \div \frac{1}{5} = 4$

TRY

Divide. $\frac{5}{6} \div \frac{1}{12}$

Problem Solving

READ

A board is $\frac{2}{3}$ yard long. Jenna cuts the board into pieces that are $\frac{1}{6}$ yard long. How many pieces are there?

PLAN

Find how many groups of $\frac{1}{6}$ are in $\frac{2}{3}$.

Divide. $\frac{2}{3} \div \frac{1}{6}$

SOLVE

To divide, multiply by the reciprocal of the divisor.

$\frac{2}{3} \div \frac{1}{6} = \frac{2}{3} \times \frac{6}{1} =$ _____

Write the product in simplest form. _____

CHECK

Use models to check.

$\frac{1}{3}$		$\frac{1}{3}$			
$\frac{1}{6}$	$\frac{1}{6}$	$\frac{1}{6}$	$\frac{1}{6}$		

Explain how the models justify the **quotient**.

_____

_____

▶ Jenna cut the board into _____ pieces.

Practice

Draw models to help you to find the quotient.

1. $\dfrac{3}{5} \div \dfrac{2}{10} =$ _____

 HINT Find how many groups of $\dfrac{2}{10}$ are in $\dfrac{3}{5}$.

2. $\dfrac{1}{2} \div \dfrac{1}{8} =$ _____

3. $\dfrac{3}{4} \div \dfrac{3}{12} =$ _____

Write the related multiplication problem for each division problem.

4. $\dfrac{7}{8} \div \dfrac{2}{3}$

5. $\dfrac{3}{10} \div \dfrac{5}{6}$

6. $\dfrac{4}{5} \div \dfrac{1}{2}$

_____   _____   _____

REMEMBER Multiply by the reciprocal of the divisor.

7. $\dfrac{5}{12} \div \dfrac{3}{4}$

8. $\dfrac{7}{9} \div \dfrac{5}{8}$

9. $\dfrac{9}{10} \div \dfrac{4}{9}$

_____   _____   _____

Divide. Write the quotient in simplest form.

10. $\dfrac{7}{12} \div \dfrac{2}{3}$

11. $\dfrac{2}{3} \div \dfrac{5}{6}$

12. $\dfrac{1}{8} \div \dfrac{2}{5}$

_____   _____   _____

13. $\dfrac{9}{25} \div \dfrac{4}{5}$

14. $\dfrac{3}{20} \div \dfrac{7}{10}$

15. $\dfrac{4}{15} \div \dfrac{3}{5}$

_____   _____   _____

16. $\dfrac{5}{12} \div \dfrac{3}{5}$

17. $\dfrac{3}{10} \div \dfrac{11}{20}$

18. $\dfrac{7}{25} \div \dfrac{2}{3}$

_____   _____   _____

Choose the best answer.

19. Divide. $\frac{1}{3} \div \frac{1}{2}$

    A. $\frac{1}{6}$

    B. $\frac{2}{5}$

    C. $\frac{2}{3}$

    D. $1\frac{1}{2}$

20. $\frac{2}{3} \div \frac{8}{9} = \square$

    A. $\frac{5}{9}$

    B. $\frac{16}{27}$

    C. $\frac{3}{4}$

    D. $1\frac{1}{3}$

Solve.

21. How many $\frac{1}{6}$-pound hamburgers can be made from $\frac{1}{2}$ pound of hamburger meat?

_____

22. A relay race is $\frac{4}{5}$ mile long. Each runner runs $\frac{1}{10}$ mile. How many runners are in the relay?

_____

23. A piece of string is $\frac{3}{4}$ meter long. How many pieces of string that are $\frac{1}{20}$ meter long can Wyatt cut?

_____

24. Julia has $\frac{3}{4}$ quart of orange juice. She will fill each glass with $\frac{3}{16}$ quart of juice. How many glasses can she fill?

_____

25. CONCLUDE Why is $\frac{1}{2}$ of $\frac{1}{8}$ different than $\frac{1}{2} \div \frac{1}{8}$?

_____

_____

_____

26. DECIDE Which is greater: $\frac{1}{9} \div \frac{2}{3}$ or $\frac{2}{3} \div \frac{1}{9}$? Explain why.

_____

_____

_____

LESSON

8 Problem Solving: Dividing with Fractions

Water Stations

READ

A race is 3 miles long. There are water stations every $\frac{3}{4}$ mile along the route. How many water stations are along the route?

PLAN

Write an equation to represent the problem.

Let n = the number of water stations.

$3 \div \frac{3}{4} = n$

SOLVE

Write the division problem as a _____ problem.

Multiply the dividend by the _____ of the divisor.

$3 \div \frac{3}{4} = 3 \times$ _____

Write the whole number as an improper fraction.

Then multiply. Write the product in simplest form.

$3 \times$ _____ = _____ $\times$ _____ = _____ = _____

$3 \div \frac{3}{4} =$ _____

CHECK

Explain how the models below justify the quotient.

1				1				1			
$\frac{1}{4}$	$\frac{1}{4}$	$\frac{1}{4}$	$\frac{1}{4}$	$\frac{1}{4}$	$\frac{1}{4}$	$\frac{1}{4}$	$\frac{1}{4}$	$\frac{1}{4}$	$\frac{1}{4}$	$\frac{1}{4}$	$\frac{1}{4}$

$\frac{3}{4}$ $\frac{3}{4}$ $\frac{3}{4}$ $\frac{3}{4}$

_____

_____

▶ There are _____ water stations along the route.

Frame It

A rectangular frame that is $\frac{2}{3}$ foot long has an area of $\frac{5}{18}$ square foot. How wide is the frame?

PLAN

The area of a rectangle is length multiplied by width.

So the width is equal to the area divided by the _____.

Write an equation to represent the problem.

Let w = the width of the frame.

$$w = \frac{5}{18} \div \frac{2}{3}$$

SOLVE

To solve the equation, multiply the dividend by the _____ of the divisor.

$$\frac{5}{18} \div \frac{2}{3} = \underline{} \times \underline{}$$

Multiply. Write the product in simplest form.

$$\underline{} \times \underline{} = \underline{} = \underline{}$$

$$w = \underline{}$$

CHECK

Use the relationship between multiplication and division to check the quotient.

Because multiplication and division are opposite operations, the product of the quotient multiplied by the divisor should equal the dividend.

If $\frac{5}{18} \div \frac{2}{3} =$ _____, then _____ $\times \frac{2}{3} = \frac{5}{18}$.

Check the product.

$$\underline{} \times \frac{2}{3} = \underline{} = \underline{}$$

So, $\frac{5}{18} \div \frac{2}{3} =$ _____, because _____ $\times \frac{2}{3} = \frac{5}{18}$.

▶ The frame is _____ foot wide.

Practice

Use the 4-step problem-solving process to solve each problem.

1. **READ** Setsuko has a rectangular piece of fabric that is $\frac{5}{6}$ yard wide. The area of the fabric is $\frac{5}{16}$ square yard. How long is Setsuko's fabric?

   PLAN _____

   _____

   SOLVE

   CHECK

2. How much trail mix will each person get if 6 people share $\frac{3}{4}$ pound of trail mix equally?

3. A potter has 9 pounds of clay. He uses $\frac{3}{10}$ pound of clay for each bowl he makes. How many bowls can the potter make?

4. How long is a rectangular field with a width of $\frac{3}{5}$ mile and an area of $\frac{21}{50}$ square mile?

5. How many $\frac{1}{2}$ cup servings of rice are in $\frac{3}{8}$ cup of rice? Explain why your answer is reasonable.

LESSON 9

Dividing Whole Numbers

EXAMPLE A Divide. 29,745 ÷ 6

1

The first digit of the quotient will be in the thousands place. Divide the 29 thousands by 6.

That is 4 thousands in each group.

```
      4
6)29745
  -24        ←  4 × 6
    5        ←  29 − 24
```

There are 5 thousands left.

2

Bring down the 7. Divide the 57 hundreds by 6.

That is 9 hundreds in each group.

```
     49
6)29745
  -24↓
    57
   -54       ←  9 × 6
     3       ←  57 − 54
```

There are 3 hundreds left.

3

Bring down the 4. Divide the 34 tens by 6.

That is 5 tens in each group.

```
    495
6)29745
  -24↓
    57
   -54↓
     34
    -30      ←  5 × 6
      4      ←  34 − 30
```

There are 4 tens left.

4

Bring down the 5. Divide the 45 ones by 6.

That is 7 ones in each group.

```
    4957 R3
6)29745
  -24↓
    57
   -54↓
     34
    -30↓
      45
     -42     ←  7 × 6
       3     ←  45 − 42
```

The **remainder** is 3 ones. Write it next to the quotient.

▶ 29,745 ÷ 6 = 4,957 R3

CHECK

Check your answer using multiplication. Remember to add the remainder.

EXAMPLE B Divide. 173,264 ÷ 34

1

Set up the problem.

$$34\overline{)173264}$$ $\Box$ ← There are not enough ten thousands to divide by 34, so the first digit is in the thousands place.

2

Divide the 173 thousands by 34.

That is 5 thousands in each group.

```
        5
34)173264
  -170        ← 5 × 34
    3         ← 173 − 170
```

3

Bring down the 2. There are not enough hundreds to divide, so write 0 in the quotient in the hundreds place.

```
       50
34)173264
  -170↓
    32
```

4

Bring down the 6. Divide the 326 tens by 34.

That is 9 tens in each group.

```
       509
34)173264
  -170↓↓
    326
   -306       ← 9 × 34
     20       ← 326 − 306
```

5

Bring down the 4. Divide the 204 ones by 34.

That is 6 ones in each group.

```
       5096
34)173264
  -170↓↓
    326
   -306↓
     204
    -204      ← 6 × 34
       0      ← 204 − 204
```

▶ 173,264 ÷ 34 = 5,096

CHECK

Use multiplication to check your answer.

EXAMPLE C It cost $258,336 to make 18 antennas. How much did it cost to make each antenna?

Divide. $258,336 \div 18 = n$ $18\overline{)258336}$

1

Decide where to place the first digit in the quotient.

$$\begin{array}{r} \square \\ 18\overline{)258336} \end{array}$$ ← The first digit will be in the ten thousands place.

2

Divide.

$$\begin{array}{r} 1\,4\,3\,5\,2 \\ 18\overline{)258336} \\ -18\downarrow \\ \hline 78 \\ -72\downarrow \\ \hline 63 \\ -54\downarrow \\ \hline 93 \\ -90\downarrow \\ \hline 36 \\ -36 \\ \hline 0 \end{array}$$

← 1 × 18
← Subtract. Bring down the 8 thousands. Divide the 78 thousands.
← 4 × 18
← Subtract. Bring down the 3 hundreds. Divide the 63 hundreds.
← 3 × 18
← Subtract. Bring down the 3 tens. Divide the 93 tens.
← 5 × 18
← Subtract. Bring down the 6 ones. Divide the 36 ones.
← 2 × 18
← Subtract.

3

Estimate to check that the answer is reasonable.

Use **compatible numbers** to estimate the quotient.
258,336 is about 300,000
18 is close to 20.

A reasonable estimate of the quotient is 300,000 ÷ 20.
300,000 ÷ 20 = 15,000

14,352 is close to 15,000, so the answer is reasonable.

▶ It cost $14,352 to make each antenna.

Why might you prefer to use an estimate to check that a quotient is reasonable instead of using multiplication to check the answer?

Division Sentence Search

Each dividend can be divided by one of the divisors to create one of the quotients. Match the divisors and the quotient with the correct dividend to write a true division sentence.

Dividends	Divisors	Quotients
23,004	29	287
26,978	32	324
35,322	45	423
36,032	58	609
36,378	63	732
38,520	71	856
46,116	86	1,126
59,972	94	2,068

_____

_____

_____

_____

_____

_____

Practice

Estimate each quotient.

1. 59,628 ÷ 73

2. 361,245 ÷ 58

3. 104,392 ÷ 64

 HINT Compatible numbers are numbers that are easy to divide. Use 36 ÷ 6 to estimate.

Divide. Check your answer.

4. 5)16,380

5. 3)65,713

6. 7)6,846

> **REMEMBER** Divide, multiply, and subtract in each step.

7. 16)13,522

8. 40)82,920

9. 52)936,327

10. 39)201,357

11. 75)64,875

12. 81)520,101

Find each missing number.

	Dividend	Divisor	Quotient	Remainder
13.	12,516	53	236	
14.	53,381	28		13
15.		76	4,021	0
16.		49	7,154	20
17.	8,040		92	36

18. Choose a 5-digit number and a 1-digit number. Both must be greater than 1. Write a real-world problem about dividing the 5-digit number by the 1-digit number. Then solve the problem.

_____

_____

19. Write a real-world problem about dividing $145,775 by $25. Then solve the problem.

_____

_____

Solve.

20. There were 124,800 visitors to a special exhibit at the museum. The exhibit lasted 30 days. What was the daily average number of visitors to the special exhibit?

_____

21. Kristy bought a car for $26,424. She is paying for the car with 36 equal monthly payments. How much is each payment?

_____

22. A tour group spent $13,496 on airline tickets. There are 28 people in the group. How much did each person spend on an airline ticket?

_____

23. The concert hall has 25,350 seats. There are 78 rows of seats in the hall. Each row has the same number of seats. How many seats are in each row?

_____

24. **DEDUCE** How could the fact $36 \div 6 = 6$ help you estimate the quotient of $364,573 \div 64$?

_____

_____

25. **ASSESS** Sometimes a real-world problem involving division has a remainder. To complete the solution, you have to interpret the remainder. Explain why.

_____

_____

_____

10 Adding and Subtracting Decimals

EXAMPLE A Find the sum.

$$523.7 + 94.34$$

1

Line up the decimal points in the addends.

$$
\begin{array}{r}
523.7 \\
+\ 94.34 \\
\end{array}
$$

2

Use zeros as placeholders.

$$
\begin{array}{r}
523.70 \\
+\ 94.34 \\
\end{array}
$$

3

Add from right to left.

$$
\begin{array}{r}
\;1\;\;1 \\
523.70 \\
+\ 94.34 \\
\hline
618\ 04 \\
\end{array}
$$

4

Place the decimal point in the sum.

$$
\begin{array}{r}
\;1\;\;1 \\
523.70 \\
+\ 94.34 \\
\hline
618.04 \\
\end{array}
$$

▶ $523.7 + 94.34 = 618.04$

DISCUSS

Why do you line up the decimal points when you add decimal numbers?

EXAMPLE B Add.

$$265.647 + 182.095 = y$$

1

Line up the decimal points.

```
  265.647
+ 182.095
```

2

Add.

```
 1    11
  265.647
+ 182.095
  447 742
```

3

Place the decimal point in the sum.

```
 1    11
  265.647
+ 182.095
  447.742
```

4

Estimate to check that the sum is reasonable.

Round each addend to the nearest hundred.

265.647 rounds to 300.

182.095 rounds to 200.

The estimated sum is about 300 + 200, or 500.

The exact sum, 447.742, is close to 500.

So the sum is reasonable.

▶ $y = 447.742$

TRY

Add.

$$9.736 + 0.86 = w$$

EXAMPLE C Find the difference.

$$375.6 - 118.26$$

1

Set up the problem to subtract vertically.
Line up the decimal points.

```
  375.6
-118.26
```

2

Use zeros as placeholders.

```
  375.60
-118.26
```

3

Subtract from right to left.

```
     6 15   5 10
  3 7̶ 5̶ . 6̶ 0̶
- 1 1 8 . 2 6
  2 5 7   3 4
```

4

Place the decimal point in the difference.

```
     6 15   5 10
  3 7̶ 5̶ . 6̶ 0̶
- 1 1 8 . 2 6
  2 5 7 . 3 4
```

5

Estimate to check that the sum is reasonable.

Round each addend to the nearest hundred.

375.6 rounds to 400.

118.26 rounds to 100.

The difference is about 400 − 100, or 300.

The exact difference, 257.34, rounds to 300.

So the difference is reasonable.

▶ 375.6 − 118.26 = 257.34.

TRY

Subtract.

$$28.61 - 9.8 = d$$

🛠 Problem Solving

READ

At the tournament, Team A scored 192.586 points. Team B scored 170.399 points. How many more points did Team A score than Team B?

PLAN

Write an equation to represent the problem.

Let p = the difference between the two team's points.

$192.586 - 170.399 = p$

SOLVE

Line up the decimal points.

Then subtract.

$$
\begin{array}{r}
192.586 \\
-170.399 \\
\hline
\end{array}
$$

CHECK

Use addition to check the answer.

Line up the decimal points in the addends.

Does the total equal Team A's points? _____

▶ Team A scored _____ more points than Team B.

Practice

Add or subtract. Check your answer.

1.
```
  4.98
+72.65
```

2.
```
 425.2
-173.45
```

3.
```
 57.93
+43.2
```

4.
```
 7.328
-0.76
```

 HINT To subtract in each place, add a zero to 425.2 as a placeholder.

5.
```
 329.45
+156.28
```

6.
```
 138.4
- 48.732
```

7.
```
 27.629
+16.83
```

8.
```
 52.521
-38.89
```

9. $12.3 + 5.427$

10. $5.189 - 2.94$

11. $328.25 + 42.78$

REMEMBER Align the decimal point to add or subtract in the same place.

12. $72.9 + 6.437$

13. $513.98 - 85.39$

14. $472.6 + 8.352$

15. $0.83 + 56.7$

16. $8.2 - 0.684$

17. $16 - 2.361$

Find the missing number.

18. $3.982 - \underline{\hspace{2cm}} = 1.74$

19. $\underline{\hspace{2cm}} + 739.2 = 953.16$

20. $62.31 + \underline{\hspace{2cm}} = 100.8$

21. $\underline{\hspace{2cm}} - 39.04 = 82.752$

22. $50.06 - \underline{\hspace{2cm}} = 18.123$

23. $29.8 - \underline{\hspace{2cm}} = 6.082$

Choose the best answer.

24. Allie rode her bike 4.3 kilometers from home to the park, She rode for 7.85 kilometers around the park. Then she rode back home along her original route. How many kilometers did Allie ride in all?

   A. 8.28 km

   B. 8.71 km

   C. 12.15 km

   D. 16.45 km

25. Mark's batting average is 0.34. Last year, it was 0.175. By how much has Mark's batting average increased?

   A. 0.141

   B. 0.165

   C. 0.175

   D. 0.515

26. Write a real-world problem that can be solved by adding two decimals. Then solve the problem.

_____

Solve.

27. A diver scores 6.892, 7.935, 6.253, and 8.025 in four dives. What is the diver's total score?

   _____

28. Kanye has to drive 193 miles to visit his grandparents. He drives 85.46 miles and then stops to get gas. How many miles does Kanye have left to drive?

   _____

29. CONCLUDE When you compute with decimals, you should always check that your answer is reasonable. Why?

   _____

   _____

30. JUSTIFY Why do you always line up the decimal points when you add or subtract decimal numbers?

   _____

   _____

11 Multiply and Divide Decimals

EXAMPLE A Find the product.

5.27 × 31.84

1

Multiply as with whole numbers.

```
    4   2
    1
  1 5   2
  3 1 . 8 4
×     5 . 2 7
  2 2 2 8 8
  6 3 6 8 0
+1 5 9 2 0 0 0
  1 6 7 7 9 6 8
```

2

Count the decimal places in the factors. Add.

Put the total number of decimal places in the product.

```
    3 1 . 8 4   ← 2 decimal places
×       5 . 2 7   ← 2 decimal places
  1 6 7 . 7 9 6 8   ← 4 decimal places
```

3

You can also estimate the product to place the decimal point.

The product is about 30 × 5, or 150.

167.7968 is closer to 150 than 16.77968 or 1677.968.

▶ 5.27 × 31.84 = 167.7968

TRY

Find each product.

52.7 × 31.84

52.7 × 318.4

EXAMPLE B A bag of pears weighs 6.75 pounds. The pears cost $2.39 per pound. What is the total cost of the pears?

Multiply.

$6.75 \times \$2.39 = c$

1

Multiply as with whole numbers.

```
    2   5
    2   6
    1   4
  $ 2 . 3 9
×   6 . 7 5
    1 1 9 5
  1 6 7 3 0
+ 1 4 3 4 0 0
  1 6 1 3 2 5
```

2

Place the decimal point in the product.

$$\begin{array}{r} \$2.39 \\ \times\ \ 6.75 \\ \hline 16.1325 \end{array}$$ ← 2 decimal places
← 2 decimal places
← 4 decimal places

3

Check that the product is reasonable.

The product is about 2×7, or 14.

14 is close to 16.1325, so the product is reasonable.

4

Find the cost to the nearest cent.

Round the product to the hundredths place.

16.13<u>2</u>5 ← The digit to the right of the hundredths place is less than 5. Round down.

To the nearest cent, 16.1325 rounds to 16.13.

▶ The total cost of the pears is $16.13.

DISCUSS

Why do you round money amounts to the nearest hundredth?

EXAMPLE C Divide.

$$16.15 \div 0.38$$

1

Make the divisor a whole number by multiplying the divisor and the dividend by 100.

$0.38\overline{)16.15}$ $0.38 \times 100 = 38$

$16.15 \times 100 = 1615$

$0.38\overline{)16.15} \longrightarrow 38\overline{)1615}$

2

Place the decimal point in the quotient.

Place the decimal point above the decimal point in the dividend.

$38\overline{)1\,6\,1\,5.}$

3

Divide as with whole numbers.

```
        4 2.
38)1 6 1 5.
  -1 5 2↓      ← 4 × 38
      9 5      ← Subtract. Bring down the 5 ones. Divide the 95 ones.
    -7 6       ← 2 × 38
      1 9      ← Subtract.
```

4

Place a zero in the tenths place in the dividend and continue to divide.

```
        4 2.5
38)1 6 1 5.0
  -1 5 2↓ |
      9 5  |
    -7 6  ↓
      1 9 0    ← Bring down the 0 tenths. Divide the 190 tenths.
    -1 9 0    ← 5 × 38
          0
```

▶ $16.15 \div 0.38 = 42.5$

CHECK

Use multiplication to check your answer.

```
    4 2.5
  × 0. 3 8
```

⚙ Problem Solving

READ

Nima drove 187.68 kilometers in 3.2 hours. What was her average speed?

PLAN

Write an equation to represent the problem.

Let k = the number of kilometers Nima drove each hour.

$187.68 \div 3.2 = k$

SOLVE

Make the divisor a whole number by multiplying the divisor and the dividend by 10.

$3.2 \times 10 =$ _____

$187.68 \times 10 =$ _____

Place the decimal point in the quotient.

Divide as with whole numbers.

Divide until there is no remainder.

$$32 \overline{)1\,8\,7\,6.8\,0}$$

CHECK

$$\frac{}{\times\ \ 3.2}$$

The quotient, k, is _____.

▶ Nima drove at an average speed of _____ kilometers per hour.

Practice

Write the number of decimal places that will be in the product.

1. 4.18×0.7 **2.** 96×1.23 **3.** 72.06×3.12 **4.** 67.3×275

_____   _____   _____   _____

 HINT Add the number of decimal places in the factors.

Rewrite each problem so that the divisor is a whole number.

5. $287.6 \div 4.2$ **6.** $45.56 \div 0.18$ **7.** $673.29 \div 5.6$

_____   _____   _____

REMEMBER Multiply the divisor and the dividend by the same multiple of ten.

Find the product. Check that your answer is reasonable.

8. 36×2.56 **9.** 1.9×42.5 **10.** 5.7×8.4

_____   _____   _____

11. 8.46×0.53 **12.** 7.36×21.4 **13.** 56.92×42.09

_____   _____   _____

Find the quotient. Check your answer.

14. $1.29 \div 0.3$ **15.** $248.43 \div 6.5$ **16.** $6.74 \div 2.5$

_____   _____   _____

17. $0.45\overline{)3.78}$ **18.** $8.2\overline{)141.86}$ **19.** $0.06\overline{)19.2}$

20. When you divide a decimal by a number greater than 1, how does the quotient compare with the dividend? When you divide a decimal by a number less than 1, how does the quotient compare with the dividend? Give examples to support your answer.

_____

21. Write a real-world problem that can be solved by multiplying two decimals. Then solve the problem.

_____

22. Write a real-world problem that can be solved by dividing two decimals. Then solve the problem.

_____

Solve.

23. Andie bought 4.85 meters of cord. The cord cost $0.98 per meter. What was the total cost of the cord?

_____

24. Naomi drove 710.24 miles on 18.4 gallons of gas. How many miles per gallon did her car get?

_____

25. Sameer worked for 6.2 hours each day for 5 days. He earned $18.75 per hour. How much did Sameer earn in all?

_____

26. Ming bought 9.8 gallons of gas for $37.73. How much did she pay per gallon?

_____

27. (PROVE) Explain how to find the product of 0.03×2.06. How do you know that the product is reasonable?

_____

_____

_____

28. (SUMMARIZE) Explain how to divide a decimal by a decimal.

_____

_____

_____

LESSON 12 Extending Factors and Multiples to GCF and LCM

UNDERSTAND You can use area models or grids to find the **greatest common factor (GCF)** of two numbers.

Find the GCF of 8 and 20.

1

Think of 8 and 20 as the dimensions of a rectangle.
To find the GCF using models, find the dimensions of the largest square that can tile the entire rectangle with no gaps or overlaps.
The largest square that fits inside the rectangle is a square against one side with length 8 units long. Two 8 by 8 squares fit inside the rectangle. However, they do not fill the rectangle.

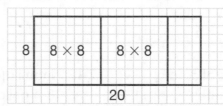

2

The largest square that fits inside the remaining rectangle is a 4 by 4 square. Two 4 by 4 squares fit and completely fill the original rectangle.

Since the original rectangle is now filled, 4 is the GCF.

3

Notice that the entire 8 by 20 rectangle can be filled with the 4 by 4 squares.

▶ The GCF of 8 and 20 is 4.

⊸€ Connect

Find the GCF of 8 and 20.

1

List all the **factors** of each number.

Factors of 8: 1, 2, 4, 8

Factors of 20: 1, 2, 4, 5, 10, 20

2

Find the common factors of 8 and 20.

Underline the common factors.
These are the factors in both lists.

Factors of 8: 1, 2, 4, 8

Factors of 20: 1, 2, 4, 5, 10, 20

3

Find the GCF.

Find the greatest factor that appears in both lists.

Factors of 8: 1, 2, 4, 8

Factors of 20: 1, 2, 4, 5, 10, 20

4 is the greatest factor that appears in both lists.

▶ The GCF of 8 and 20 is 4.

MODEL

Use an area model to find the GCF of 6 and 15.

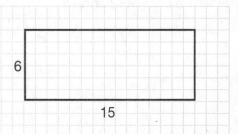

EXAMPLE A The GCF of two numbers is 3. The two numbers are between 35 and 46. The greater number has two more factors than the lesser number. What are the numbers?

1

Decide which of the numbers between 35 and 46 have 3 as a factor.

Is 3 a factor of:

36? Yes	41? No
37? No	42? Yes
38? No	43? No
39? Yes	44? No
40? No	45? Yes

2

List the factors of 36, 39, 42, and 45.

36: 1, 2, 3, 4, 6, 9, 12, 18, 36

39: 1, 3, 13, 39

42: 1, 2, 3, 6, 7, 14, 21, 42

45: 1, 3, 5, 9, 15, 45

3

Which pairs of numbers have 3 as the GCF?

36 and 39? Yes

36 and 42? No

36 and 45? No

39 and 42? Yes

39 and 45? Yes

42 and 45? Yes

4

The greater number has two more factors than the lesser number.

Does 39 have 2 more factors than 36? No

Does 42 have 2 more factors than 36? No

Does 45 have 2 more factors than 36? No

Does 42 have 2 more factors than 39? No

Does 45 have 2 more factors than 39? Yes

Does 45 have 2 more factors than 42? No

▶ The numbers are 39 and 45.

TRY

Find the GCF of 12 and 18.

EXAMPLE B Use the **distributive property** to express the sum below.

$54 + 12$

1

Find the GCF of 54 and 12.

List the factors of 54 and 12.

Factors of 54: 1, 2, 3, <u>6</u>, 9, 18, 27, 54

Factors of 12: 1, 2, 3, 4, <u>6</u>, 12

The GCF of 54 and 12 is 6.

2

Write each addend with 6 as a factor.

$54 = 6 \times 9$

$12 = 6 \times 2$

3

Rewrite the expression as a sum with the factors.

$54 + 12 = (6 \times 9) + (6 \times 2)$

4

Use the distributive property.

Use the GCF as the factor that is distributed to each term in the sum.

$(6 \times 9) + (6 \times 2) = 6(9 + 2)$

▶ $54 + 12 = 6(9 + 2)$

CHECK

How do you know that the equation $54 + 12 = 6(9 + 2)$ is true?

EXAMPLE C Find the **least common multiple (LCM)** of 6 and 9.

1

List some **multiples** of each number.

Multiples of 6: 6, 12, 18, 24, 30, 36, 42, 48, 54

Multiples of 9: 9, 18, 27, 36, 45, 54

2

Find the common multiples.

Underline the common multiples. These are the multiples found in both lists.

Multiples of 6: 6, 12, <u>18</u>, 24, 30, <u>36</u>, 42, 48, <u>54</u>

Multiples of 9: 9, <u>18</u>, 27, <u>36</u>, 45, <u>54</u>

3

Find the LCM.

Find the least multiple that appears in both lists.

Multiples of 6: 6, 12, <u>18</u>, 24, 30, <u>36</u>, 42, 48, <u>54</u>

Multiples of 9: 9, <u>18</u>, 27, <u>36</u>, 45, <u>54</u>

18 is the least multiple that appears in both lists.

▶ The LCM of 6 and 9 is 18.

DISCUSS

How can you choose when to stop while making a list of multiples to find the LCM?

Solve the Riddles

1 The GCF of two numbers less than or equal to 12 is 2. Their LCM is 20. What are the numbers?

_____

2 The LCM of two numbers less than or equal to 12 is 36. The GCF of the numbers is 3. What are the numbers?

_____

3 The GCF of two numbers is 4. The numbers are between 10 and 20. What are the numbers?

_____

4 The LCM of two numbers less than or equal to 12 is 30 more than 12. What are the numbers?

_____

5 The GCF of two numbers less than 100 is 12. The difference between the numbers is 36. The greater number is a multiple of 10. What are the numbers?

_____

6 Write your own GCF riddle. Exchange your riddle with classmates and solve.

_____

_____

7 Write your own LCM riddle. Exchange your riddle with classmates and solve.

_____

_____

_____

Practice

Use area models or grids to find the GCF of each pair of numbers.

1. 4, 10

2. 6, 12

3. 9, 15

 HINT The lesser number can always form at least one square.

Find the GCF of each pair of numbers.

4. 5, 20

5. 9, 24

6. 7, 10

7. 18, 42

8. 14, 35

9. 15, 60

10. 24, 40

11. 25, 45

12. 16, 18

Find the LCM of each pair of numbers.

13. 4, 12

14. 5, 7

15. 2, 10

16. 6, 8

REMEMBER The first multiple of a number is the number itself.

17. 3, 5

18. 4, 7

19. 5, 6

20. 4, 9

21. 8, 12

22. 3, 10

23. 9, 12

24. 2, 11

Use the distributive property to express each sum with the GCF factored out.

25. $45 + 30$

_____

26. $16 + 28$

_____

27. $32 + 56$

_____

28. $24 + 39$

_____

29. $50 + 75$

_____

30. $35 + 20$

_____

Solve.

31. Consider the numbers between 20 and 30. Which number has the greatest number of factors?

_____

32. What is the GCF of 12, 20, and 36?

_____

33. What is the LCM of 3, 4, and 8?

_____

34. Find the GCF and the LCM of 9 and 12.

_____

35. Tristan has 45 apples and 20 pears that he is putting into gift baskets. Each basket will have the same number of apples and pears. What is the greatest number of baskets Tristan can make with no fruit left over? Explain.

_____

_____

36. At Poultry Paradise, turkey burgers are sold in packages of 8. Whole-grain buns are sold in packages of 6. What is the least number of turkey burgers and buns Carly can buy to have an equal number of each? Explain.

_____

_____

37. DEMONSTRATE What is the least common factor of any pair of numbers? Explain.

_____

_____

_____

38. ANALYZE Why are you able to find a greatest common factor but not a greatest common multiple?

_____

_____

_____

Locating Positive and Negative Integers on a Number Line

Negative numbers are less than zero and are located to the left of 0 on a horizontal number line. **Positive numbers** are greater than zero and are located to the right of 0.

EXAMPLE A Locate 9 and its **opposite** on a number line.

The number line shows positive and negative **integers**. The integer 9 can be written as 9 or +9. The opposite of a number lies the same distance from 0 on a number line but in the other direction. The opposite of 9 is −9.

To plot a point at 9, count 9 units to the right of 0 and draw a point.

To plot a point at −9, count 9 units to the left of 0 and draw a point.

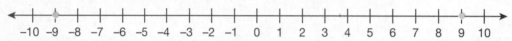

▶ The number line above shows the location of 9 and its opposite, −9.

EXAMPLE B Find the opposite of the opposite of −6.

1

Find the opposite of −6.

The opposite of −6 is the integer with the opposite sign that lies the same distance from 0. The opposite of a negative number is a positive number.
So the opposite of −6 is 6.

2

Find the opposite of the opposite of −6.

The opposite of −6 is 6. To find the opposite of the opposite, find the opposite of 6. The opposite of 6 is −6.

▶ The opposite of the opposite of −6 is −6.

DISCUSS

What number is its own opposite? Explain.

EXAMPLE C In a football game, the team with possession of the ball gained 35 yards. What is the opposite of gaining 35 yards?

1 Decide what 0 means in the situation.

In this situation, 0 is the place on the field where the team with possession starts. From that point, the team gained 35 yards.

2 Write the opposite of 35 as an integer.

The opposite of 35 is -35.

3 Interpret the meaning of -35 yards.

The number -35 yards means losing 35 yards from 0, the place on the field where the team with possession starts.

▶ The opposite of gaining 35 yards is -35 yards or losing 35 yards.

EXAMPLE D The low temperature in a 24-hour period was $-7°F$. What is the opposite of $-7°F$?

1 Decide what 0 means in the situation.

In this situation, 0 is the point on the temperature scale that separates the positive temperatures from the negative temperatures. Positive temperatures are above 0, and negative temperatures are below 0.

2 Interpret the meaning of $-7°F$ in this situation.

In this situation, $-7°F$ means $7°F$ below 0.

3 Find the opposite of $-7°F$.

The opposite of $-7°F$ is $7°F$.

In this situation, $7°F$ means 7 degrees above 0.

▶ The opposite of $-7°F$ is $7°F$ or $7°F$ above 0.

TRY

What is the opposite of $32°F$?

Practice

Locate each integer and its opposite on a number line. What is each integer's location in relation to 0? Use *Math Tool: Blank Number Lines.*

1. 4 _____

2. −7 _____

3. −18 _____

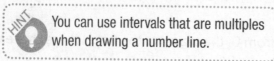

HINT You can use intervals that are multiples when drawing a number line.

4. 50 _____

Find the opposite of the opposite of each number.

5. −2   6. 15   7. 43   8. −38   9. −100

_____   _____   _____   _____   _____

REMEMBER Find the opposite. Then find the opposite of the opposite.

10. What is the opposite of the opposite of any integer? How do you know?

_____

Write an integer to represent each situation.

11. 30 feet below sea level   12. 1°C below 0   13. gaining 6 points

_____   _____   _____

14. a bank deposit of $40   15. a loss of 3 yards in a football game   16. a debit of $5

_____   _____   _____

Write an integer to represent each situation. Explain the meaning of 0 in the situation. Then describe the opposite situation, and write an integer to represent it.

17. Going up 6 flights of stairs

_____

18. A $25 withdrawal from an account

_____

19. Losing 8 pounds

_____

20. A credit of $10

_____

21. A $200 loss in an investment

_____

22. 82 meters above sea level

_____

Solve.

23. WRITE MATH Describe a situation that can be represented by the integer 20 and its opposite.

_____

_____

24. ARGUE Why is it important to understand the meaning of 0 when using integers to represent real-world situations?

_____

_____

LESSON 14 Understanding Absolute Value

EXAMPLE A Evaluate $|-8|$.

1 Understand the notation.

Write: $|-8|$

Read: the **absolute value** of -8

2 Locate -8 on a number line.

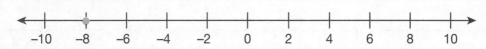

3 Use the definition of absolute value to evaluate $|-8|$.

The absolute value of a number is its distance from 0.

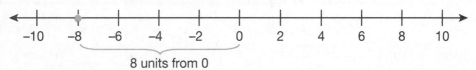

8 units from 0

-8 is 8 units from 0.

▶ $|-8| = 8$

DISCUSS

Why is the absolute value of a number always greater than or equal to 0?

EXAMPLE B A submarine is cruising at −65 feet. How many feet below the surface is the submarine?

1

Use absolute value to represent the situation.

The problem asks for the distance of the submarine from the surface.

Find |−65|.

2

Evaluate |−65|.

The absolute value of a number is its distance from 0.

−65 is 65 units to the left of 0 on a number line.

So |−65| = 65.

3

Interpret the meaning of the absolute value.

The absolute value represents the distance of the submarine from the surface. Since a distance is always greater than or equal to 0, the location of the submarine is a positive distance from the surface.

▶ The submarine is located 65 feet below the surface.

TRY

A weather balloon records data at 1,000 feet above the ocean. How many feet above sea level is the weather balloon?

EXAMPLE C Audrey has an account balance less than −$24. Is her debt greater than or less than $24?

1

Locate −24 on a number line.

2

Evaluate |−24|.

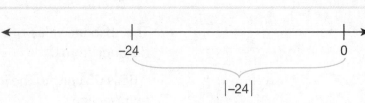

|−24| = 24

3

Use the number line to show an amount less than −24.

An account balance less than −$24 means that Audrey's debt is greater than $24.

▶ Audrey's debt is greater than $24.

Thatcher has an account balance of more than −$10. Is his debt greater than or less than $10? Explain.

⚙ Problem Solving

Yoshiro returned a shirt to the store. He received a credit of $15 to spend at the store. If he spends $20, will the credit cover the purchase?

Use integers to represent the credit and the amount spent.

Use absolute value to compare the credit amount to the amount Yoshiro spends.

What is the credit amount as an integer? _____

What is the amount Yoshiro spends as an integer? _____

What is the absolute value of the credit amount? _____

What is the absolute value of the amount Yoshiro spends? _____

Compare the absolute value of the credit amount to the absolute value of the amount Yoshiro spends. _____

Does the $15 credit cover the $20 purchase? _____

How do you know that your answer is reasonable?

_____

▶ The $15 credit _____ cover the $20 purchase.

Practice

Evaluate the absolute value of each integer.

1. $|7|$ **2.** $|-4|$ **3.** $|21|$ **4.** $|-10|$

_____   _____   _____   _____

 HINT The absolute value of an integer is its distance from 0 on a number line.

5. $|52|$ **6.** $|-64|$ **7.** $|-99|$ **8.** $|-126|$

_____   _____   _____   _____

What values can _n_ have to make each equation true?

9. $|n| = 3$ **10.** $|n| = 14$ **11.** $|n| = 1$

_____   _____   _____

> **REMEMBER** Distance can be measured to the left of 0 or to the right of 0 on a number line.

12. $|n| = 0$ **13.** $|n| = 76$ **14.** $|n| = 189$

_____   _____   _____

Use absolute value to represent each situation. Then solve.

15. The lake reaches a depth of -85 meters. How many meters below the surface is the lake bottom?

_____

16. Mr. Murray had a return of $-\$110$ on a stock investment. What was Mr. Murray's loss on the stock?

_____

17. A liquid freezes at a temperature of $-63°F$. How many degrees below 0 does the liquid freeze?

_____

18. An airplane is flying at an elevation of 52,000 feet. How many feet above sea level is the airplane flying?

_____

Solve.

19. Izabella has an account balance of more than −$6. Is her debt greater than or less than $6? Explain.

_____

_____

20. Sterling has an account balance less than −$40. Is his debt greater than or less than $40? Explain.

_____

_____

21. Phoebe has an account balance more than −$15. How does her debt compare to a debt of $20? Explain.

_____

_____

22. Hector has a credit of $45 to spend at a bicycle shop. If he spends $38, will the credit cover the purchase? Explain.

_____

_____

23. Write a problem with a real-world context using |−10|.

_____

_____

_____

24. Write a problem with a real-world context using |36|.

_____

_____

_____

25. CONCLUDE Which is the greater debt: −$3 or −$30? Use absolute value to explain.

_____

_____

_____

26. DEFINE Explain what the absolute value of an integer is.

_____

_____

_____

Locating Rational Numbers on a Number Line

EXAMPLE A Locate $-1\frac{3}{4}$ on the number line.

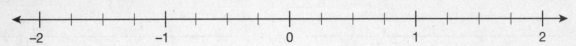

1

Decide if the point lies to the left of 0 or to the right of 0.

Negative **rational numbers** lie to the left of 0 on a horizontal number line.

The number $-1\frac{3}{4}$ is negative, so it lies to the left of 0.

2

Count $1\frac{3}{4}$ units to the left of 0 to locate the point.

The number line is divided into fourths.

Each interval to the left of 0 represents $-\frac{1}{4}$.

Start at 0.

Count 4 fourths from 0 to -1.

Then count 3 more fourths from -1 to $-1\frac{3}{4}$.

Plot a point at $-1\frac{3}{4}$.

Label the point.

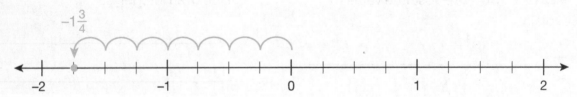

▶ The number line above shows $-1\frac{3}{4}$ on the number line.

MODEL

Locate $1\frac{1}{4}$ on the number line.

EXAMPLE B A stock fell 3.6 points. Plot the amount the stock fell on a number line.

1

Write a rational number to represent the situation.

Let 0 represent the starting value of the stock.

Since the stock fell, its value is less than the starting value.

The rational number −3.6 represents the amount the stock fell.

2

Draw a number line.

−3.6 is between −3 and −4.

Draw a horizontal number line divided into tenths from −4 to −3.

Label the integers.

3

Locate −3.6 on the number line.

Start at −3 and count 0.6 units to the left.

Plot a point at −3.6.

Label the point.

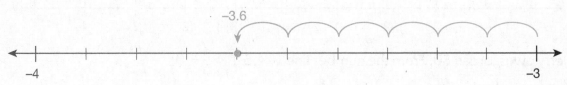

▶ The number line above shows −3.6, the amount the stock fell.

DISCUSS

How is locating −3.6 on a number line different than locating 3.6 on a number line? How is it similar?

EXAMPLE C Jerry owed Jordan $4.50. Jerry paid back Jordan $4.50. How much does Jerry still owe Jordan?

1

Use rational numbers to represent how much Jerry owed Jordan and how much Jerry paid him back.

Jerry owed Jordan $4.50: −4.5

Jerry paid Jordan back $4.50: 4.5

2

Locate −4.5 on a number line.

−4.5 is between −4 and −5. From −4, count 0.5 units to the left. Plot and label a point.

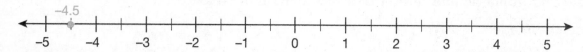

3

Use the same number line to determine how much Jerry owes Jordan.

Jerry paid back $4.50. Jerry paid back the amount he originally owed Jordan.

From −4.5, move right 4.5 units on the number line.

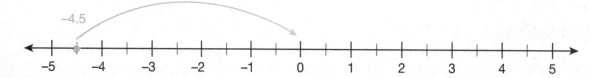

So Jerry owes Jordan $0. From the number line, −4.5 + 4.5 = 0.

▶ Jerry owes Jordan $0.

TRY

If you lose $1.25 in the morning and you find $1.25 in the afternoon, how much money did you lose in all? Explain.

EXAMPLE D From the ground, Maribel climbed $65\frac{1}{3}$ feet up a cliff face. Then she rappelled $65\frac{1}{3}$ feet down the cliff face. Where was Maribel after she rappelled down the cliff face?

1

Use rational numbers to represent how far Maribel climbed up the cliff face and how far she rappelled down.

Up: $65\frac{1}{3}$

Down: $-65\frac{1}{3}$

2

Use a number line to show how far Maribel climbed up the cliff face.

On the number line, 0 represents the ground.

Locate $65\frac{1}{3}$ on a number line.

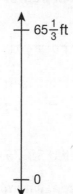

3

Use the same number line to show how far Maribel rappelled down the cliff face.

Maribel rappelled down the same distance she went up the cliff face.

$65\frac{1}{3} + \left(-65\frac{1}{3}\right) = 0$

So she is back at the place where she started.

▶ After she rappelled down the cliff face, Maribel was back on the ground.

TRY

At the entrance to a cave, Josh climbs down $10\frac{1}{2}$ feet into a chamber. Then he climbs back up $10\frac{1}{2}$ feet from the chamber. Where is Josh after he climbs back up?

Practice

Name each point on the number line below using both a fraction and a decimal.

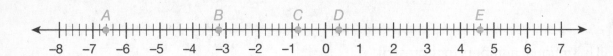

1. A
_____

2. B
_____

3. C
_____

4. D
_____

5. E
_____

> **HINT** Start at 0 and count units from right to left to name a point less than 0.

Plot and label each point on the number line below.

6. $-4\frac{1}{6}$

7. $-2\frac{2}{3}$

8. -0.5

9. $1\frac{1}{3}$

10. 2.5

11. Juliet deposited $8.75 in a checking account.

Draw a horizontal number line to show the deposit.

What does 0 mean on your number line?

_____

Juliet writes a check for $8.75. How does this change the amount from when she deposited $8.75 into the account? Why?

_____

_____

Solve.

12. From sea level, a helicopter rises to an elevation of 125.8 meters. Then it descends 125.8 meters. What is the elevation of the helicopter after it descends? Explain.

_____

_____

13. Mr. Sampson lost $5\frac{1}{4}$ pounds. Then he gained $5\frac{1}{4}$ pounds. How did Mr. Sampson's weight change from the time he lost the weight to the time he gained the weight? Explain.

_____

_____

14. In the morning a stock rises 2.85 points. By closing time the stock falls 2.85 points. Use rational numbers to record the stock changes in the morning and by closing time. How much did the stock change from the morning to closing? Explain.

_____

_____

15. From the surface, a diver descends to a depth of $32\frac{5}{6}$ feet. Then the diver rises $32\frac{5}{6}$ feet. Draw a number line to show the situation. Where is the diver when she rises to the surface? Explain.

_____

_____

16. Landon earns $16.50. He spends $16.50 for a concert ticket. How much money does Landon have left? Use a sum of rational numbers to explain.

_____

_____

17. Write a negative rational number greater than −50. Write the opposite of your rational number. Then add the number and its opposite. What is the sum?

_____

_____

18. CONTRAST How is locating a rational number on a number line similar to locating an integer? How is it different?

_____

_____

_____

19. JUSTIFY Why is the sum of a rational number and its opposite always equal to 0?

_____

_____

_____

16 Ordering Rational Numbers

EXAMPLE A Compare -2 and -5.

1

Locate each integer on a number line.

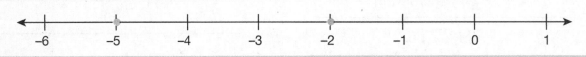

2

Compare the positions of the integers on the number line.

When oriented from left to right on the number line, -5 lies to the left of -2.

In other words, -2 lies to the right of -5.

3

Use symbols to compare the integers.

On a number line, the lesser number lies to the left of the greater number.

Since -5 lies to the left of -2, $-5 < -2$.

On a number line, the greater number lies to the right of the lesser number.

Since -2 lies to the right of -5, $-2 > -5$.

▶ So $-5 < -2$ or $-2 > -5$.

MODEL

Use a number line to compare 1 and -3.

 **EXAMPLE B** The freezing point of nitrogen is 63.14 K. The freezing point of salt water is 270.6 K. Which has a lower freezing point?

1

Compare 63.14 and 270.6.

Locate each rational number on a number line.

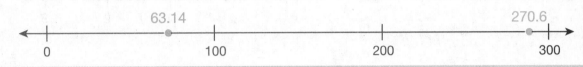

2

Use symbols to compare the rational numbers.

Use the number line to compare the numbers.

63.14 lies to the left of 270.6.
So 63.14 < 270.6.

270.6 lies to the right of 63.14.
So 270.6 > 63.14.

3

Decide which has a lower freezing point.

Since 63.14 < 270.6, nitrogen has a lower freezing point than salt water.

▶ Nitrogen has a lower freezing point than salt water.

TRY

At midnight, the temperature at the ski resort was −9.5°C. At sunrise, the temperature was 2.8°C. Use symbols to compare the temperatures. When was it warmer?

EXAMPLE C Order $-1\frac{3}{4}$, 2.6, and -4.3 from least to greatest.

1

Locate each rational number on a number line.

2

Compare the positions of the integers on the number line.

-4.3 lies to the left of $-1\frac{3}{4}$.

$-1\frac{3}{4}$ lies to the left of 2.6.

So $-4.3 < -1\frac{3}{4} < 2.6$ shows the numbers ordered from least to greatest.

Notice also that 2.6 lies to the right of $-1\frac{3}{4}$.

$-1\frac{3}{4}$ lies to the right of -4.3.

So $2.6 > -1\frac{3}{4} > -4.3$ shows the numbers ordered from greatest to least.

▶ From least to greatest, the numbers are -4.3, $-1\frac{3}{4}$, and 2.6.

MODEL

Use a number line and comparison symbols to order $1\frac{3}{8}$, 3.2, and $-1\frac{1}{2}$ from greatest to least.

Problem Solving

READ

A scientist takes temperature readings at three locations on a mountain at 8 A.M.
The temperature at the base is −10.3°C. The temperature at mid-mountain is −12°C.
The temperature at the summit is 1.8°C. Order the temperatures from greatest to least.
Which location has the warmest temperature at 8 A.M.?

PLAN

Use a number line to order the temperatures from _____ to _____.

SOLVE

Locate each temperature on a number line.

Which is the warmest temperature? How do you know?

_____

Which is the coolest temperature? How do you know?

_____

Use comparison symbols to write the temperatures from greatest to least.

_____

CHECK

How can you use your number line to support your answer?

_____

▶ From greatest to least, the temperatures are _____, _____,
and _____.

The warmest temperature at 8 A.M. was at _____.

Practice

Compare. Write > or <.

1. $-8 \bigcirc -9$

2. $0 \bigcirc -7$

3. $-4 \bigcirc \frac{1}{2}$

 HINT Compare the signs of the numbers.

4. $-3\frac{1}{8} \bigcirc -6$

5. $-1 \bigcirc -0.5$

6. $0.29 \bigcirc 0.9$

7. $6\frac{3}{4} \bigcirc -10$

8. $-1.35 \bigcirc -\frac{1}{3}$

9. $7.3 \bigcirc 7\frac{2}{3}$

10. $-6\frac{2}{5} \bigcirc -5.9$

11. $-2.8 \bigcirc -2$

12. $5\frac{4}{5} \bigcirc 5.4$

Order from least to greatest.

13. $1.75, 0, -4$

14. $-3\frac{1}{2}, -1.5, -3$

_____

_____

> **REMEMBER** You can use a number line to help order rational numbers.

15. $2\frac{5}{8}, -0.58, -2$

16. $-10.1, -1.1, -11$

_____

_____

Order from greatest to least.

17. $-4\frac{1}{6}, 6.4, -0.64$

18. $5.2, 5\frac{2}{3}, -3$

_____

_____

19. $1\frac{2}{5}, -0.2, 2.15$

20. $-6, -\frac{1}{2}, -\frac{1}{6}$

_____

_____

21. On a number line, is -2 located to the right or to the left of 3? Write two comparisons to support your answer.

_____

22. On a number line, is -6 located to the right or to the left of -9? Write two comparisons to support your answer.

_____

Write a real-world example for each inequality statement.

23. $0 > -3$

_____

24. $1\frac{2}{3} < 2\frac{1}{2}$

_____

25. $-5 > -8$

_____

26. $-2.25 < -1.5$

_____

Solve.

27. The freezing point of nitrogen is $-209.86°C$. The freezing point of mercury is $-38.87°C$. Which has a lower freezing point? Explain.

_____

28. The melting point of nitrogen is $-195.8°C$. The melting point of solid oxygen is $-218.4°C$. Which has a higher melting point? Explain.

_____

29. At opening bell, Stocks A, B, and C had the same value. By the closing bell, Stock A's value was -2.4, Stock B's value was 0.9, and Stock C's value was -3. Which stock gained the most? Which stock lost the most? Explain.

_____

_____

30. Hannah ran her first lap around the track in 50.5 seconds. She ran her second lap in 51.2 seconds. She ran her third lap in 49 seconds. Which lap was Hannah's slowest lap? Which lap was Hannah's fastest lap? Explain.

_____

_____

31. **DEMONSTRATE** Explain how to use a number line to order any three rational numbers from least to greatest. Give an example.

_____

_____

_____

32. **WRITE MATH** Explain why every positive rational number is greater than every negative rational number.

_____

_____

_____

Plotting Ordered Pairs on the Coordinate Plane

EXAMPLE A Plot $(-4, 3)$ on a coordinate plane. Which quadrant is the point located in?

1

Identify the quadrants on a coordinate plane.

Two perpendicular number lines intersect to form the **coordinate plane**. The horizontal number line is the **x-axis**. The vertical number line is the **y-axis**. The axes intersect at the **origin**. The axes divide the coordinate plane into four **quadrants**.

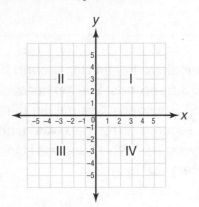

2

Plot $(-4, 3)$ on a coordinate plane.

Points on a coordinate plane can be located by **ordered pairs**. The first number of an ordered pair tells how far to move left or right from the origin. The second number tells how far to move up or down.

To plot $(-4, 3)$, start at the origin, $(0, 0)$. The first number is -4, so move 4 units to the left of 0. The second number is positive, so move 3 units up. Plot and label the point.

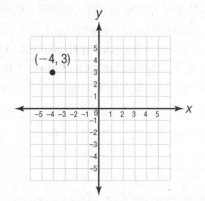

3

Locate the quadrant.

You can use the signs of the numbers in an ordered pair to find the quadrant.

Quadrant I: $(+, +)$ Quadrant II: $(-, +)$
Quadrant III: $(-, -)$ Quadrant IV: $(+, -)$

The first number in $(-4, 3)$ is negative and the second number is positive, so the point lies in Quadrant II.

▶ The point $(-4, 3)$ is shown on the coordinate plane. It lies in Quadrant II.

TRY

Plot $(2, -2)$ on the coordinate plane. Which quadrant is the point located in?

EXAMPLE B Plot (3, −5) and (−3, 5) on a coordinate plane. How are the ordered pairs different? In which quadrant is each point located?

1

Plot each point on a coordinate plane.

To plot (3, −5), start at the origin. Move 3 units to the right and 5 units down.

To plot (−3, 5), start at the origin. Move 3 units to the left and 5 units up.

Label each point.

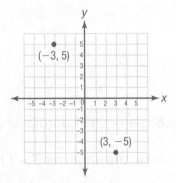

2

Compare the numbers in the ordered pairs.

The first numbers in the ordered pairs have opposite signs.

The second numbers in the ordered pairs also have opposite signs.

3

Find the quadrants where the points are located.

Because the signs of the coordinates are different, the ordered pairs lie in different quadrants.

(3, −5) is in Quadrant IV.

(−3, 5) is in Quadrant II.

▶ The points are shown on the coordinate plane. The coordinates of the ordered pairs differ by their signs. (3, −5) is in Quadrant IV, and (−3, 5) is in Quadrant II.

TRY

Plot (3, 5) and (−3, −5) on the coordinate plane. Which quadrant is each point located in?

EXAMPLE C From Zoe's house, the hospital is 2 blocks to the east and 4 blocks south. Her school is $3\frac{1}{2}$ blocks to the west and 1 block south. The park is $2\frac{1}{2}$ blocks to the west and $2\frac{1}{2}$ blocks north. The library is 4 blocks to the east and $\frac{1}{2}$ block north. Plot the locations of the hospital, school, park, and library on a coordinate grid in relation to Zoe's house.

1

Write an ordered pair for each location.

Zoe's house lies at the origin. Each unit represents 1 block.

East lies to the right of the origin, and west lies to the left of the origin.

North lies above the origin, and south lies below the origin.

Hospital: $(2, -4)$ School: $\left(-3\frac{1}{2}, -1\right)$

Park: $\left(-2\frac{1}{2}, 2\frac{1}{2}\right)$ Library: $\left(4, \frac{1}{2}\right)$

2

Plot each point on a coordinate grid.

Plot a point at the origin for Zoe's house.

Then plot the points to show the locations of each place. Label what each point represents.

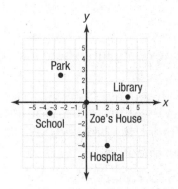

▶ The coordinate grid above shows the location of the hospital, school, park, and library in relation to Zoe's house.

MODEL

A grocery store is 1 unit west and $4\frac{1}{2}$ units south of Zoe's house. Plot and label a point to show the grocery store on the coordinate grid.

EXAMPLE D Reflect rectangle *ABCD* across the *y*-axis.

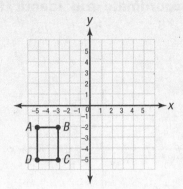

1 Decide how the coordinates of an ordered pair change when the point is reflected across the *y*-axis.

When a point is reflected across the *y*-axis, the point lies on the opposite side of the *y*-axis. This means that the first number in the ordered pair changes its sign and the second number stays the same.

2 Write the ordered pairs of each reflected point.

Each point is reflected across the *y*-axis. Change the sign of the first number in the original point to write the ordered pair of the reflection.

Use a prime ′ to represent the reflection.

Ordered Pairs

Point	Reflection
$A(-5, -2)$	$A'(5, -2)$
$B(-3, -2)$	$B'(3, -2)$
$C(-3, -5)$	$C'(3, -5)$
$D(-5, -5)$	$D'(5, -5)$

3 Plot and label the reflection of each point. Connect the points to form a rectangle.

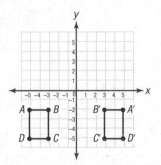

▶ The reflection of rectangle *ABCD* is rectangle *A′ B′ C′ D′*. It is shown on the above grid.

How do the coordinates of an ordered pair change when the point is reflected across the *x*-axis? Explain.

Practice

Plot and label each point on the coordinate grid. Identify the quadrant where the point is located.

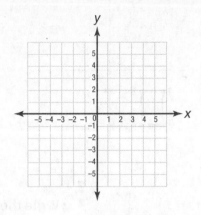

1. $C(-1, -1)$ **2.** $D(2, -4)$ **3.** $E(1.5, 3)$ **4.** $F(-5, 1)$ **5.** $G\left(4, -4\frac{1}{2}\right)$

_____   _____   _____   _____   _____

 HINT   1.5 is between 1 and 2.

Identify the quadrant where each ordered pair is located.

6. $(2, 4)$

_____

7. $(-2, 4)$

_____

8. $(10, 5)$

_____

> REMEMBER You can use a coordinate grid to find the quadrant.

9. $(-6, -9)$

_____

10. $\left(1\frac{3}{4}, -1\frac{2}{3}\right)$

_____

11. $(0.5, -0.5)$

_____

12. $(-25, 5)$

_____

13. $(8.75, 12)$

_____

14. $(-19, -40)$

_____

15. $(325, -200)$

_____

16. $(-123, -361)$

_____

17. $(-0.75, 1.5)$

_____

18. From the park, Harun's house is 3 blocks to the west and 3 blocks south. Eli's house is 2 blocks to the west and 4 blocks north. Lily's house is 2 blocks to the east and 1 block north. Elena's house is 5 blocks to the east and 4 blocks south. Plot the locations of the Harun's, Eli's, Lily's, and Elena's houses on the coordinate grid in relation to the park.

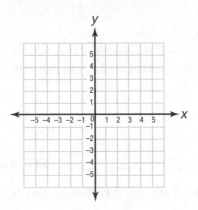

19. Reflect trapezoid *CDEF* across the y-axis.

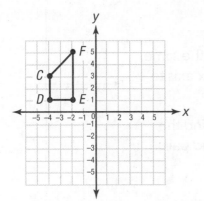

20. Reflect parallelogram *JKLM* across the x-axis.

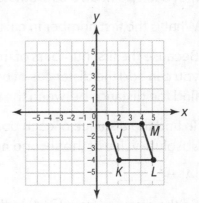

Solve.

21. (INTERPRET) When the first number in an ordered pair is 0, where is the point located? When the second number in an ordered pair is 0, where is the point located? How do you know?

_____

_____

_____

Problem Solving: Using the Coordinate Plane

Library Walk

READ

On a coordinate plane, a school is located at (2, 4). The library is located at (2, −3). If each unit on the plane represents one block, how far does Kyle walk to go to the library after school?

PLAN

Plot the points _____ and _____ on a coordinate plane.

Use absolute value to find the distance between the points.

SOLVE

Plot each point on a coordinate plane.

What is the first number in each ordered pair? _____

Because the first numbers of the ordered pairs are the same, you can add the distances of both points from the *x*-axis to find the distance between the points.

To find the distance of each point from the *x*-axis, find the absolute value of the second number in the ordered pair.

$|4| =$ _____ $|-3| =$ _____

So the distance from (2, 4) to the *x*-axis is _____ units.

The distance from (2, −3) to the *x*-axis is _____ units.

Add the absolute values to find the distance between the points.

_____ + _____ = _____

How many blocks away from the school is the library? _____

CHECK

Count the vertical units between the points.

How many vertical units from (2, 4) to (2, −3)? _____

▶ Kyle walks _____ blocks to go to the library after school.

From Luke to Leah

READ

Each unit on the coordinate plane below represents one mile. The ordered pair for Luke's house is $(4, -3)$. Leah's house is west of Luke's house. Luke and Leah live 9 miles apart. What ordered pair represents Leah's house?

PLAN

Plot the point for Leah's house _____ units west of Luke's house.

SOLVE

Plot a point at _____ for Luke's house.

Because Leah's house is west of Luke's house, count _____ units to the _____ to reach Leah's house.

Plot a point for Leah's house at _____.

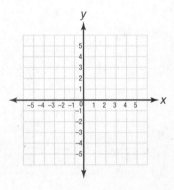

CHECK

Find the distance between the points. Are the second coordinates in the ordered pairs the same? _____

Because the second coordinates in the ordered pairs are the same, add the distances of both points from the y-axis to find the distance between the points.

To find the distance of each point from the y-axis, find the absolute value of the first coordinates in the ordered pairs.

Find each absolute value. _____

Add the absolute values. _____ + _____ = _____

What is the distance between the points? _____

Is Leah's house 9 miles from Luke's house? _____

▶ The ordered pair for Leah's house is _____.

Practice

Use the 4-step problem-solving process to solve each problem.

1. **READ**   On a coordinate plane map, the soccer stadium is located at $(-1, 8)$. The bus stop is located at $(6, 8)$. If each unit represents one block, how far will Renata have to walk from the bus stop to the stadium?

    PLAN _____

    _____

    SOLVE

    CHECK

2. Each unit on a coordinate plane represents one kilometer. One end of a street starts at $(-30, -5)$. The street ends at $(10, -5)$. How long is the street?

3. An artist draws a square on a coordinate plane. The coordinates of two corners on the square are (1, 2) and (−2, −1). The sides of the square are 3 units long. What are the coordinates of the other two corners on the square?

4. Each unit on a coordinate plane represents one mile. The mall is at (−16, 15). Colt's office is 18 miles due south of the mall. What are the coordinates of Colt's office on the grid?

5. On a coordinate plane, Akira's house is located at (−12, 9). Her dance studio is located at (−12, −7). If each unit represents one block, how far is it from Akira's house to her dance studio?

Divide. Write the quotient in simplest form.

1. $\frac{5}{8} \div \frac{3}{4}$ _____

2. $\frac{3}{4} \div 2$ _____

3. $\frac{3}{5} \div \frac{7}{10}$ _____

4. $\frac{12}{25} \div \frac{3}{5}$ _____

Add or subtract. Check your answer.

5. $9.63 + 4.567$

6. $8.6 - 2.43$

7. $126.78 - 87.9$

8. $4.73 + 0.947$

9. $78 - 35.23$

10. $8.062 + 1.76$

Find the product. Check that your answer is reasonable.

11. 3.8×1.56

12. 0.7×82.5

13. 4.1×7.6

14. 2.34×0.96

Find the quotient. Check your answer.

15. $18{,}472 \div 8$

16. $94{,}198 \div 13$

17. $37.4 \div 5.5$

18. $34\overline{)18{,}632}$

19. $0.28\overline{)4.48}$

20. $4.3\overline{)32.25}$

Find the GCF of each pair of numbers.

21. 12, 30

22. 8, 64

23. 15, 24

_____

_____

_____

Find the LCM of each pair of numbers.

24. 5, 8

25. 3, 12

26. 4, 10

_____

_____

_____

Use the distributive property to express each sum with the GCF factored out.

27. $35 + 63$

28. $48 + 18$

_____

_____

Write an integer to represent each situation. Explain the meaning of 0 in the situation. Then describe the opposite situation, and write an integer to represent it.

29. 25 feet below sea level

_____

30. 5°F above 0

_____

31. a gain of 8 points

_____

Find the opposite of the opposite of each number.

32. -8

33. 35

34. 110

35. -97

_____

_____

_____

_____

36. On a number line, is -4 located to the right or to the left of 3? Write two comparisons to support your answer.

_____

37. On a number line, is −3 located to the right or to the left of −1? Write two comparisons to support your answer.

_____

Write the quadrant where each ordered pair is located.

38. (4, −6)   **39.** (−9, −1)   **40.** (5, 3)   **41.** (−2, 8)

_____   _____   _____   _____

Write the location of each point on the number line below using both a fraction and a decimal.

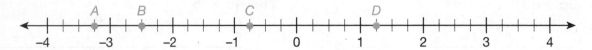

42. A   **43.** B   **44.** C   **45.** D

_____   _____   _____   _____

Solve.

46. How wide is a rectangular table with a length of $\frac{2}{3}$ yard and an area of $\frac{1}{2}$ square yard?

_____

47. Harry has an account balance of more than −$8. Is his debt greater than or less than $8?

_____

48. The surface temperature on Mars can range from −17.2°C to −107°C. Which temperature is lower?

_____

49. Each unit on a coordinate plane represents one mile. One end of a road starts at (−12, −3). The road ends at (6, −3). How long is the road?

_____

DECODE the ORDERED PAIRS

Step 1: Use *Math Tool: Coordinate Planes.*
Plot 4 points in different quadrants.

Step 2: Code the ordered pairs. For each point,
write clues for each coordinate in the ordered pair.

Clues may include operations, factors, multiples, opposites, and absolute values.

> For example: The first coordinate in this ordered pair is the opposite of the GCF of 8 and 12.
> The second coordinate is the quotient of $2.5 \div 0.5$. The ordered pair is $(-4, 5)$.

Step 3: Exchange clue sets with a classmate, and decode the ordered pairs.
Plot the points on another coordinate plane and compare solutions.

_____

_____

_____

_____

_____

_____

_____

_____

_____

_____

_____

_____

Grade 5 OA

Write and interpret numerical expressions.

Analyze patterns and relationships.

Grade 7 RP

Analyze proportional relationships and use them to solve real-world and mathematical problems.

Grade 6 EE

Apply and extend previous understandings of arithmetic to algebraic expressions.

Reason about and solve one-variable equations and inequalities.

Represent and analyze quantitative relationships between dependent and independent variables.

Grade 7 EE

Use properties of operations to generate equivalent expressions.

Solve real-life and mathematical problems using numerical and algebraic expressions and equations.

Grade 5 NF

Apply and extend previous understandings of multiplication and division to multiply and divide fractions.

Grade 7 G

Solve real-life and mathematical problems involving angle measure, area, surface area, and volume.

Domain 3
Expressions and Equations

Writing and Evaluating Numerical Expressions

EXAMPLE A Write a **numerical expression** for $8 \times 8 \times 8$ using an **exponent**.

1

Identify the **base** in the **expression**.

The base or repeated factor is 8.

$\underline{8} \times \underline{8} \times \underline{8}$

2

Identify the exponent.

$8 \times 8 \times 8$ ← There are three 8s.

So the exponent is 3.

3

Write the expression using an exponent.

8^3

▶ Using an exponent, $8 \times 8 \times 8$ can be written as 8^3.

EXAMPLE B Expand the expression.

9^4

1

Identify the base and the exponent in the expression.

In 9^4, the base is 9 and the exponent is 4.

TRY

Use an exponent to write an expression for $2 \times 2 \times 2 \times 2 \times 2$.

2

Expand the expression.

The base, 9, is repeated 4 times.

$9 \times 9 \times 9 \times 9$

▶ The expression 9^4 can be written as $9 \times 9 \times 9 \times 9$.

EXAMPLE C Use the **order of operations** to evaluate the expression.

$$6 \times (2 + 3)^3$$

1

Do the operations within parentheses first.

$6 \times (2 + 3)^3 \quad \leftarrow \quad 2 + 3 = 5$

6×5^3

2

Evaluate the exponent.

$6 \times 5^3 \quad \leftarrow \quad 5^3 = 5 \times 5 \times 5 = 125$

6×125

3

Multiply and divide from left to right.

$6 \times 125 \quad \leftarrow \quad 6 \times 125 = 750$

750

▶ The value of the expression $6 \times (2 + 3)^3$ is 750.

EXAMPLE D Evaluate the expression.

$$7^2 + 16 \div 4 - 3$$

1

Evaluate the exponent.

$7^2 + 16 \div 4 - 3 \quad \leftarrow \quad 7^2 = 7 \times 7 = 49$

$49 + 16 \div 4 - 3$

2

Multiply and divide from left to right.

$49 + 16 \div 4 - 3 \quad \leftarrow \quad 16 \div 4 = 4$

$49 + 4 - 3$

3

Add and subtract from left to right.

$49 + 4 - 3 \quad \leftarrow \quad 49 + 4 = 53$

$53 - 3$

50

▶ $7^2 + 16 \div 4 - 3 = 50$

TRY

Evaluate the expression.

$78 - 2^3 \div 4$

Practice

Write each expression using an exponent.

1. $5 \times 5 \times 5 \times 5$

_____

2. 7×7

_____

3. $4 \times 4 \times 4 \times 4 \times 4 \times 4$

_____

 HINT Count the number of times the factor is multiplied.

Expand each expression.

4. 6^3

_____

5. 3^5

_____

6. 8^4

_____

REMEMBER The exponent tells how many times to repeat the factor.

Evaluate each expression.

7. 9^2

_____

8. 2^6

_____

9. 6^3

_____

10. 4^4

_____

11. 10^3

_____

12. 12^2

_____

Evaluate each expression.

13. $4^2 + 5^2$

_____

14. $38 - 32 \div 4 + 2^4$

_____

15. $100 \div (4 + 1)^2$

_____

16. $8 \times 3^2 - 6 \times 3$

_____

17. $4^3 \div 2 + 9$

_____

18. $63 - 6^2 \div 2$

_____

19. $4 \times (1 + 2)^3 + 5$

_____

20. $250 - 2^4 + 9^2$

_____

Choose the best answer.

21. Which shows the expression using an exponent?

$3 \times 3 \times 3 \times 3 \times 3$

A. 3^5

B. 5^3

C. 53

D. 35

22. Which shows how to expand 7^4?

A. 74

B. 7×4

C. $4 \times 4 \times 4 \times 4 \times 4 \times 4 \times 4$

D. $7 \times 7 \times 7 \times 7$

23. What is the value of the expression?

$100 - 9^2 \div 3$

A. 6

B. 30

C. 73

D. 97

24. Which expression has a value of 4?

A. $12 \div 2^2 + 2$

B. $24 \div (2 + 1) - 2^2$

C. $16 \div (1 + 1)^2 - 1$

D. $36 \div (2 + 2) - 3^2$

25. What is the value of the expression?

$2 + 6 \times 3^2$

A. 56

B. 72

C. 83

D. 326

26. What is the value of the expression?

$3 \times 4^2 - 2 \times 6$

A. 12

B. 36

C. 132

D. 276

Solve.

27. EXAMINE Is the value of $3 \times 3 \times 3 \times 3 \times 3 \times 3$ the same as the value of 3^5? Explain.

_____

28. ANALYZE Explain how to use the order of operations to evaluate the expression.
$2 \div 2 + 2 \times 2^2 - 2$

_____

_____

Reading and Writing Algebraic Expressions

LESSON 20

EXAMPLE A Write an **algebraic expression** to represent "8 less than four times a number."

1

Choose a **variable** for the number. Write four times the number as one of the **terms**.

Let n = the number

four times n

$4 \times n$ or $4n$

The **coefficient** of $4n$ is 4. The coefficient tells you to multiply the number by 4.

2

Identify the operation.

The phrase *less than* indicates subtraction.

8 *less than* means to subtract 8 from $4n$.

3

Write the expression.

8 *less than* four times a number

$4n \ - \ 8$

▶ An algebraic expression to represent "8 less than four times number" is $4n - 8$.

TRY

Write an algebraic expression to represent "6 more than twice a number."

EXAMPLE B Write a verbal expression for the algebraic expression $x \div 3 + 4$.

1 Understand the first operation used in the expression.

$x \div 3$ means a number, x, divided by 3.

2 Understand the second operation used in the expression.

$+ 4$ means add 4.

3 Use the operations to write a verbal expression.

4 more than a number divided by 3

▶ A verbal expression to represent $x \div 3 + 4$ is "4 more than a number divided by 3" or "a number divided by 3 plus 4."

TRY

Write a verbal expression for the algebraic expression $3m - 5$.

EXAMPLE C Write an algebraic expression for the verbal expression "4 times the sum of 3 and m."

1

This expression has two terms. Write an algebraic expression for "the sum of 3 and m."

Identify the operation.

To find the sum, you need to add.

$3 + m$ or $m + 3$

2

Write an algebraic expression for "4 times $3 + m$."

Use parentheses to group the addition expression.

$4 \times (3 + m)$

▶ An algebraic expression for "4 times the sum of 3 and m" is $4 \times (3 + m)$ or $4(3 + m)$.

DISCUSS

The second factor in $3(8 - m)$ is the difference of two terms. What are the two terms?

Problem Solving

READ

Holly read twice as many books as Amber read this month. Amber read 3 more books this month than last month. Write an algebraic expression for the number of books Holly read this month.

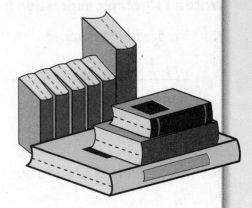

PLAN

Step 1: Write an expression for the number of books Amber read this month.

Let b = number of books Amber read last month

Step 2: Write an expression for the number of books Holly read this month.

SOLVE

Step 1: This month, Amber read $b +$ _____ books.

Step 2: Holly read twice as many books as Amber this month.

This month, Holly read _____ $\times$ ($b +$ _____) books.

CHECK

Does the expression match the verbal description in the problem? _____

▶ An algebraic expression for the number of books Holly read this month is _____.

Holly read _____ books this month.

Practice

Write an algebraic expression for each verbal expression. Let x = the number.

1. 5 more than a number

_____

2. 10 decreased by a number

_____

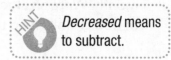
HINT *Decreased* means to subtract.

3. the quotient of 12 and a number

_____

4. 8 times a number

_____

5. subtract 9 from a number

_____

6. multiply a number by 7

_____

7. divide a number by 20

_____

8. the sum of 15 and a number

_____

Write a verbal expression for each algebraic expression.

9. $12s$

_____

10. $y - 3$

_____

REMEMBER The coefficient is a factor of the product.

11. $6 + k$

_____

12. $p \div 5$

_____

13. $8 - m$

_____

14. $32 \div x$

_____

Write an algebraic expression for each verbal expression. Let n = the number.

15. the product of 4 and the sum of 6 and a number _____

16. 5 more than the quotient of a number and 2 _____

17. the sum of 14 and the product of 8 and a number _____

Choose the best answer.

18. Which algebraic expression represents the verbal expression "subtract 3 from x"?

  A. $3 + x$

  B. $3 - x$

  C. $x - 3$

  D. $3x$

19. Which algebraic expression represents the verbal expression "the sum of 8 and the quotient of n and 2"?

  A. $8 + (n - 2)$

  B. $8 + (n \div 2)$

  C. $8(n - 2)$

  D. $8(n \div 2)$

20. Which verbal expression represents the algebraic expression $10 \div b$?

  A. the sum of 10 and b

  B. 10 multiplied by b

  C. subtract 10 from b

  D. divide 10 by b

21. Which algebraic expression does **not** show a product?

  A. $y + 2$

  B. $8y$

  C. $5(6 - y)$

  D. $2(y + 1)$

Solve.

22. Jonathan had some DVDs. He gave 6 of them away. Write an algebraic expression for the number of DVDs Jonathan has left.

_____

23. A clown made 3 times as many balloon hats as balloon dogs. He made 4 more balloon dogs than balloon swords. Write an algebraic expression for the number of balloon hats the clown made.

_____

24. CONCLUDE In the algebraic expression $7 \div y$, what is the coefficient of y? Explain.

_____

_____

_____

25. WRITE Describe a situation that can be written as an algebraic expression. Explain what the variable in your expression represents.

_____

_____

_____

Evaluating Algebraic Expressions

EXAMPLE A Evaluate $42 \div 6 + 8x$ for $x = 9$.

1

Substitute 9 for x in the expression.

$42 \div 6 + 8x$

$42 \div 6 + 8(9)$

2

Use the order of operations to evaluate the expression.

$42 \div 6 + 8(9)$	←	Divide. $42 \div 6 = 7$
$7 + 8(9)$	←	Multiply. $8(9) = 72$
$7 + 72$	←	Add.
79		

▶ When $x = 9$, $42 \div 6 + 8x$ is equal to 79.

TRY

Evaluate the expression $42 \div 6 + 8x$ for $x = \frac{1}{2}$.

EXAMPLE B Evaluate $32b - 3c - 5$ for $b = \frac{3}{4}$ and $c = 4$.

1

Substitute $\frac{3}{4}$ for b in the expression.

$32b - 3c - 5$

$32\left(\frac{3}{4}\right) - 3c - 5$

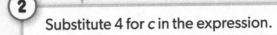

2

Substitute 4 for c in the expression.

$32\left(\frac{3}{4}\right) - 3c - 5$

$32\left(\frac{3}{4}\right) - 3(4) - 5$

3

Use the order of operations to evaluate the expression.

$32\left(\frac{3}{4}\right) - 3(4) - 5$ ← Multiply. $32\left(\frac{3}{4}\right) = 24$

$24 - 3(4) - 5$ ← Multiply. $3(4) = 12$

$24 - 12 - 5$ ← Subtract. $24 - 12 = 12$

$12 - 5$ ← Subtract.

7

▶ The value of the expression $32b - 3c - 5$ when $b = \frac{3}{4}$ and $c = 4$ is 7.

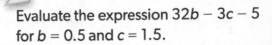

TRY

Evaluate the expression $32b - 3c - 5$ for $b = 0.5$ and $c = 1.5$.

EXAMPLE C What is the area of the triangular scarf?

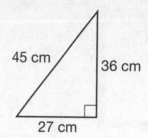

45 cm

36 cm

27 cm

1

Write an expression to represent the area.

$\frac{1}{2}bh$

In the expression, b represents the base and h represents the height of the triangle.

2

From the diagram, identify the values for the base and the height.

$b = 27$ cm

$h = 36$ cm

3

Substitute 27 cm for b and 36 cm for h in the expression.

$\frac{1}{2}(27\text{ cm})(36\text{ cm})$

4

Evaluate the numerical expression for the area.

$\frac{1}{2}(27\text{ cm})(36\text{ cm})$

$\frac{1}{2} \times 972\text{ cm}^2$

486 cm^2

▶ The area of the scarf is 486 cm².

DISCUSS

What is the area of a triangle with a height of 6 inches and a base of 12 inches?

Problem Solving

READ

Lauren's bedroom is shaped like a rectangle. She wants to carpet the entire floor.

A diagram of the floor is shown below.

12 ft

18 ft

How many square feet of carpeting does she need?

PLAN

You need to find the area of the rectangle.

The area is represented by the expression lw, where l = length and w = width.

From the diagram, identify the values for the length and the width.

l = 18 ft

w = 12 ft

Substitute the measures of the length and width in the expression.

SOLVE

Substitute 18 ft for l and _____ ft for w in the expression.

lw

18 ft × _____ ft

18 ft × _____ ft = _____ ft^2

The area of Lauren's bedroom floor is _____ ft^2.

CHECK

12 ft × 18 ft = _____ ft^2

▶ Lauren needs _____ square feet of carpeting for her bedroom floor.

Practice

Evaluate the algebraic expression for the given value of the variable.

1. $3d - 12$ for $d = 10$

_____

2. $9 + \frac{n}{4}$ for $n = 64$

_____

3. $x^2 - 6$ for $x = 7$

_____

 Evaluate the exponent first.

4. $8k - 9 \div 3$ for $k = \frac{7}{8}$

_____

5. $20 + y^2$ for $y = 8$

_____

6. $100 - 3c + 9$ for $c = \frac{2}{3}$

_____

7. $15a - 7 \times 4 + 6$
for $a = 2.4$

_____

8. $7.8 + 3.5w - 1.5$
for $w = 6.8$

_____

9. $26 + 6.4 \div 1.6 - 2b$
for $b = 3.7$

_____

Evaluate each algebraic expression for $x = 2.5$ and $y = 4$.

10. $8x + 20y$

_____

11. $6y - 4x$

_____

REMEMBER Use the order of operations to evaluate after substitution.

12. $9 + 7x - 2y$

_____

13. $12y - 3x + 5.6$

_____

14. $52 - x + y$

_____

15. $y^2 - 10 \div 5 + x$

_____

Evaluate the algebraic expression for the given values of the variables.

16. $9a - 6b$ for $a = 8$ and $b = 4$

_____

17. $75.4 - 3x + 5y$ for $x = 1.9$ and $y = 2.1$

_____

18. $10w + 9x - 4$ for $w = 3\frac{1}{2}$ and $x = \frac{2}{3}$

_____

19. $16p - 2q + 2^3$ for $p = \frac{5}{8}$ and $q = 3$

_____

Choose the best answer.

20. What is the value of the expression $3x + y$ when $x = 2$ and $y = 4$?

    A.   9

    B. 10

    C. 18

    D. 24

21. What is the area of a square with a side length of 12 centimeters? Use the expression s^2, where s is the side length of the square.

    A.   24 square centimeters

    B.   48 square centimeters

    C.   144 square centimeters

    D. 1,212 square centimeters

Solve.

22. This expression, $1.8C + 32$, shows how to convert from degrees Celsius to degrees Fahrenheit, where C represents the temperature in degrees Celsius. What is the temperature in degrees Fahrenheit when the temperature is 25°C?

_____

23. The expression $\frac{5}{9}(F - 32)$ shows how to convert from degrees Fahrenheit to degrees Celsius, where F represents the temperature in degrees Fahrenheit. What is the temperature in degrees Celsius when the temperature is 113°F?

_____

24. EVALUATE The perimeter of a rectangle is represented by the algebraic expression $2l + 2w$, where l represents the length and w represents the width of the rectangle. Find the perimeter of a rectangle that has a length of 24 feet and a width of 16 feet.

_____

25. SUMMARIZE Explain how to evaluate an algebraic expression with two variables.

_____

_____

_____

Generating and Identifying Equivalent Expressions

EXAMPLE A Write an expression equivalent to $y + y + y + y + y$.

1

Identify the variable in the expression.

The variable is y.

2

Identify the number of terms in the expression.

There are 5 terms in the expression.

The coefficient of each term, y, is 1.

4

Add the terms and write an equivalent expression.

$1y + 1y + 1y + 1y + 1y$

$5y$

▶ The expression $y + y + y + y + y$ is equivalent to the expression $5y$.

3

Identify the operation.

The expression involves addition.

EXAMPLE B Write an expression equivalent to $7(4 + x)$.

1

Use the distributive property.

$7(4 + x)$

$(7 \times 4) + (7 \times x)$

2

Use the order of operations to simplify the expression.

$(7 \times 4) + (7 \times x)$

$\quad 28 + 7x$

▶ The expression $7(4 + x)$ is equivalent to the expression $28 + 7x$.

TRY

Write an expression equivalent to the expression below.

$m \times m \times m$

EXAMPLE C Write an expression equivalent to $40a - 24b$.

1 Identify the terms.

The first term is $40a$.

The second term is $24b$.

2 Find the **greatest common factor** (GCF) of the terms.

The GCF of $40a$ and $24b$ is 8.

4 Rewrite the expression, and then factor out the 8.

$40a - 24b$

$(8 \times 5a) - (8 \times 3b)$

$8(5a - 3b)$

▸ An expression equivalent to $40a - 24b$ is $8(5a - 3b)$.

3 Write each term using the GCF as a factor.

$40a = 8 \times 5a \qquad 24b = 8 \times 3b$

EXAMPLE D Are these equivalent expressions?

$4(x + 8)$ and $4x + 18 + 14$

1 Use the distributive property to simplify $4(x + 8)$.

$4(x + 8)$

$(4 \times x) + (4 \times 8)$

$4x + 32$

2 Add to simplify the second expression.

$4x + 18 + 14$

$4x + 32$

3 Compare the expressions.

The expressions $4x + 32$ and $4x + 32$ are the same.

▸ The expressions $4(x + 8)$ and $4x + 18 + 16$ are equivalent expressions.

DISCUSS

Are the expressions $2(y + 5)$ and $2y + 2 + 5$ equivalent? Explain.

Practice

Write an equivalent expression for each expression.

1. $x + x$

_____

2. $c + c + c + c$

_____

3. $p \times p$

_____

Identify the operation.

4. $y \times y \times y \times y$

_____

5. $n + n + n + n + n$

_____

6. $a \times a \times a \times a \times a$

_____

Use the distributive property to write an equivalent expression for each expression.

7. $4(x + 3)$

_____

8. $6(4 + 2a)$

_____

9. $3(3c - d)$

_____

10. $7(5x + 12)$

_____

11. $5(2m - 4n)$

_____

12. $8\left(6y + \dfrac{5}{8}\right)$

_____

Use the GCF to write an equivalent expression for each expression.

13. $2y + 4$

_____

14. $27 + 3x$

_____

15. $10c - 15$

_____

16. $32r + 4s$

_____

17. $12c + 42d$

_____

18. $24x - 40y$

_____

Are the two expressions equivalent? Write *yes* or *no*.

19. $7(x + 2y)$ and $14x + 14y$ _____

20. $3c - 9d$ and $3(c - 3d)$ _____

21. $5(6a + 4b)$ and $20b + 30a$ _____

22. $y + y + 5w$ and $2(y + 3w)$ _____

Choose the best answer.

23. Which expression is equivalent to $6(4 + x)$?

    A. $10 + x$

    B. $24 + 6x$

    C. $10 + 6x$

    D. $24 + x$

24. Which expression is equivalent to $3(7b + 2c)$?

    A. $21b + 6c$

    B. $21b + 2c$

    C. $10b + 5c$

    D. $10b + 2c$

Solve.

25. **IDENTIFY** Write two equivalent expressions you could use to show the perimeter of this triangle.

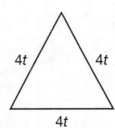

_____

26. **ANALYZE** One bookshelf is $4.1a + 3b$ inches long. Another shelf is 5 times as long. Write an expression you could use to show the length of the longer shelf.

_____

LESSON 23 Writing and Solving Equations

EXAMPLE A Is 148 a solution of the **equation** $\frac{x}{4} = 37$?

1

Understand what it means for a value to be a solution of an equation.

A value is a solution of an equation if substituting the value for the variable in the equation makes the equation true.

2

Substitute 148 for x in the equation.

$$\frac{x}{4} = 37$$

$$\frac{148}{4} \stackrel{?}{=} 37 \quad \leftarrow \quad \text{Write "?" over the equal sign.}$$

3

Evaluate $\frac{148}{4}$.

$$\frac{148}{4} = 148 \div 4 = 37$$

4

Compare the expressions on both sides of the equation.

In a true equation, the expressions on both sides of the equal sign have the same value.

Since $\frac{148}{4} = 37$ and $37 = 37$, the equation is a true equation.

▶ Yes, 148 is a solution of the equation $\frac{x}{4} = 37$.

DISCUSS

Explain why 152 is not a solution of the equation $\frac{x}{4} = 37$.

EXAMPLE B Are any of the following numbers a solution of the equation $35 = y - 16$?
19, 21, 41, 51

1

Substitute 19 for y in the equation.

$35 = y - 16$

$35 \stackrel{?}{=} 19 - 16$ ← Substitute 19 for y.

$35 \stackrel{?}{=} 3$ ← Simplify the right side of the equation.

$35 \neq 3$ ← 19 is not a solution.

2

Substitute 21 for y in the equation.

$35 = y - 16$

$35 \stackrel{?}{=} 21 - 16$ ← Substitute 21 for y.

$35 \stackrel{?}{=} 5$ ← Simplify the right side of the equation.

$35 \neq 5$ ← 21 is not a solution.

3

Substitute 41 for y in the equation.

$35 = y - 16$

$35 \stackrel{?}{=} 41 - 16$ ← Substitute 41 for y.

$35 \stackrel{?}{=} 25$ ← Simplify the right side of the equation.

$35 \neq 25$ ← 41 is not a solution.

4

Substitute 51 for y in the equation.

$35 = y - 16$

$35 \stackrel{?}{=} 51 - 16$ ← Substitute 51 for y.

$35 \stackrel{?}{=} 35$ ← Simplify the right side of the equation.

$35 = 35$ ← The equation is true. 51 is a solution.

▶ The solution to the equation is 51.

TRY

Are any of the following numbers a solution of the equation $35 = y + 16$?
19, 21, 41

EXAMPLE C Logan has 28 model cars. His grandparents give him some more model cars. Now he has 31 model cars. How many model cars did Logan's grandparents give him?

1

Choose a variable.

Let c = the number of model cars Logan's grandparents gave him.

2

Write an equation.

$28 + c = 31$

3

To solve an addition equation, use the **inverse operation**.

Addition and subtraction are inverse operations because they "undo" each other. You can find the value of c by subtracting 28 from both sides.

This will get c by itself on one side and the value of c on the other side.

$$28 + c = 31$$
$$28 - 28 + c = 31 - 28 \quad \leftarrow \quad \text{Subtract 28 from both sides of the equation.}$$
$$c = 3 \quad \leftarrow \quad \text{Simplify both sides of the equation.}$$

4

Check the equation.

Substitute 3 for c in the equation.

$$28 + c = 31$$
$$28 + 3 \stackrel{?}{=} 31$$
$$31 = 31 \quad \leftarrow \quad \text{The equation is true.}$$
$$\text{The solution is 3.}$$

▶ Logan's grandparents gave him 3 model cars.

MODEL

Write an equation for the following problem.

Deanne worked 25 hours this week. That was 3 hours less than she worked last week. How many hours did she work last week?

⚙️ Problem Solving

READ

Keke did 72 sit-ups at the end of the month. This was 6 times as many sit-ups as she was able to do at the beginning of the month. How many sit-ups was Keke able to do at the beginning of the month?

PLAN

Choose a variable. Write an equation that expresses the problem situation.

Use the inverse operation to solve the equation.

SOLVE

Let s = _____

$6s$ = _____

What operation is the inverse of multiplication? _____

Divide both sides of the equation by _____ to solve.

$$6s = \text{_____}$$

$$\text{_____} \div \text{_____} = \text{_____} \div \text{_____}$$

$$s = \text{_____} \quad \leftarrow \quad \text{Simplify.}$$

CHECK

Substitute _____ for s in the equation.

$$6s = \text{_____}$$

$$6 \times \text{_____} \stackrel{?}{=} \text{_____}$$

$$\text{_____} = \text{_____} \quad \leftarrow \quad \text{The equation is true.}$$

The solution is _____.

▶ Keke was able to do _____ sit-ups at the beginning of the month.

Practice

Is the given value a solution of the equation? Write *yes* or *no*.

1. $36.4 + k = 64.1$; $k \stackrel{?}{=} 28.7$

_____

2. $\frac{2}{3}y = 54$; $y \stackrel{?}{=} 81$

_____

 HINT Does the value make a true equation?

3. $x - 9.6 = 32.7$; $x \stackrel{?}{=} 42.3$

_____

4. $\frac{w}{15} = 45$; $w \stackrel{?}{=} 670$

_____

Write which number is a solution of the equation.

5. $18x = 25.2$ Try: 1.2, 1.3, 1.4 _____

6. $2\frac{5}{6} + b = 6\frac{2}{3}$ Try: $3\frac{5}{6}$, $3\frac{1}{3}$, $3\frac{1}{6}$ _____

REMEMBER Test each value in the equation.

7. $y \div 23 = 7$ Try: 161, 162, 163 _____

8. $n - 4.85 = 12.6$ Try: 16.91, 17.45, 17.65 _____

Use inverse operations to solve. Check your answer.

9. $17 + k = 54$

_____

10. $43 = b - 9$

_____

11. $6y = 48$

_____

12. $m \div 5 = 8$

_____

13. $x + 49 = 94$

_____

14. $s - 36 = 28$

_____

15. $3x = 123$

_____

16. $a \div 12 = 8$

_____

17. $116 = 4n$

_____

Solve. Check your answer.

18. $54 = 6w$

19. $m \div 5 = 13$

20. $y - \frac{1}{2} = \frac{3}{8}$

_____

_____

_____

21. $675 = x + 238$

22. $\frac{s}{9} = 144$

23. $74.6 + c = 82$

_____

_____

_____

Choose the best answer.

24. Which of the following is a solution of the equation?

$$48 = 8d$$

A. $d = 6$

B. $d = 40$

C. $d = 56$

D. $d = 384$

25. Which of the following is a solution of the equation?

$$n + 17 = 51$$

A. $n = 3$

B. $n = 34$

C. $n = 68$

D. $n = 867$

Solve.

26. Tanya is 62 inches tall. She is 17 inches taller than May. Write and solve an equation to find May's height.

_____

27. Oliver earns $9 per hour. Write and solve an equation to find how many hours he must work to earn $315.

_____

28. Write a real-world problem that can be solved by the equation $y + 8 = 20$. Then solve your problem.

_____

_____

29. Write a real-world problem that can be solved by the equation $5x = 45$. Then solve your problem.

_____

_____

30. ANALYZE How does using an inverse operation help you solve an equation?

_____

_____

31. EXPLAIN When solving an equation, why do you apply the inverse of the given operation to both sides?

_____

_____

LESSON 24 Writing and Solving Inequalities

EXAMPLE A Emma needs to score at least 83 on her next social studies test to earn an A in the class. Write an **inequality** to represent the situation.

1

Choose a variable.

Let s = the score Emma needs to get on her test.

2

Choose the inequality symbol.

Inequality Symbol	Verbal Clues
<	Less than, fewer than
≤	Less than or equal to, at most
>	Greater than, more than
≥	Greater than or equal to, at least

Emma needs *at least* 83. Use the ≥ inequality symbol.

3

Write the inequality.

$s \geq 83$

4

Check that the inequality expresses the situation.

The solution set is all numbers greater than or equal to 83.

This means that Emma must score 83 or any score higher than 83 on the test.

She can score 83, 84, 85, and so on, up to and including 100, to earn an A in the class.

The inequality $s \geq 83$ expresses the situation.

▶ $s \geq 83$

TRY

Todd caught a fish that weighed less than 12 pounds. Write an inequality to represent the situation.

EXAMPLE B Are any of the following numbers in the solution set of the inequality $x + 78 \leq 115$?
28, 37, 41

1

Substitute 28 for x in the inequality.

$x + 78 \leq 115$

$28 + 78 \overset{?}{\leq} 115$ ← Substitute 28 for x.

$106 \leq 115$ ← Simplify the left side of the inequality.

The inequality is true.

28 is a solution.

2

Substitute 37 for x in the inequality.

$x + 78 \leq 115$

$37 + 78 \overset{?}{\leq} 115$ ← Substitute 37 for x.

$115 \leq 115$ ← Simplify the left side of the inequality.

The inequality is true since $115 = 115$.

37 is a solution.

3

Substitute 41 for x in the inequality.

$x + 78 \leq 115$

$41 + 78 \overset{?}{\leq} 115$ ← Substitute 41 for x.

$119 \leq 115$ ← Simplify the left side of the inequality.

The inequality is not true since $119 > 115$.

41 is not a solution.

▶ 28 and 37 are in the solution set of the inequality $x + 78 \leq 115$.

DISCUSS

How does the result of substituting 37 for x in the inequality above help you find other solutions? What are three other solutions?

EXAMPLE C Solve the inequality. Graph the solution.
$$4n > 12$$

1

Use the inverse operation to solve the inequality.

$4n > 12$

$\dfrac{4n}{4} > \dfrac{12}{4}$ ← Divide both sides of the inequality by 4.

$n > 3$ ← Simplify both sides of the inequality.

2

Check the solution set.

The solution set is all numbers greater than 3.

So numbers such as 3.8, 4.2, 5, 6, and so on are all in the solution set of the inequality.

Substitute 3.8 for n in the inequality.

$4n > 12$

$4(3.8) \overset{?}{>} 12$

$15.2 > 12$ ✓

3

Graph the solution on a number line.

Draw a number line.

An open circle around a number means that the value is not in the solution set.

A closed circle around a number means that the value is in the solution set.

Since $n > 3$, 3 is not a solution.

Draw an open circle around 3. Then shade to the right of 3.

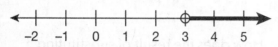

▶ The solution of the inequality is $n > 3$. The graph of the solution is shown above.

DISCUSS

How would the graph of the solution to $4n \geq 12$ be different than the graph of the solution to $4n > 12$? Explain.

⚙️ Problem Solving

READ

Write and solve an inequality that describes the problem below. Then graph the solution. Yuan walked 2 more miles than Dennis walked. Yuan walked at most 5 miles. How many miles did Dennis walk?

PLAN

Choose a variable. Write an inequality. Solve the inequality. Then graph the solution on a number line.

SOLVE

Let $m =$ _____

$m +$ _____ is the number of miles Yuan walked.

Yuan walked at most 5 miles. This means the number of miles he walked is less than or

equal to _____.

Write the inequality: $m + 2 \leq$ _____

Solve the inequality. What operation is the inverse of addition? _____

Subtract _____ from both sides of the inequality to solve.

$$m + 2 \leq \underline{\hspace{2cm}}$$

$$\underline{\hspace{2cm}} \leq \underline{\hspace{2cm}}$$

$$m \leq \underline{\hspace{2cm}}$$

Graph the solution on the number line.

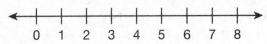

Why does the number line for the solution set start at 0? _____

CHECK

Decide if the solution set makes sense.

Dennis walked at most _____. This means he walked _____ miles or less.

Yuan walked at most 5 miles, and Dennis walked 2 fewer miles than Yuan.

▶ Dennis walked at most _____ miles.

Practice

Write an inequality for each situation. Use *x* for the variable.

1. Noah has fewer than 8 tennis balls. _____

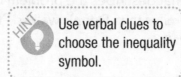

HINT Use verbal clues to choose the inequality symbol.

2. Mariposa read at least 45 pages of the book. _____

3. Jaxon rode no more than 38 miles. _____

4. Kira spent more than $85. _____

Decide whether the given value is a solution of the inequality. Write *yes* or *no*.

5. $y + 8 < 13$

    Try: $y \stackrel{?}{=} 7$

    _____

6. $7n > 105$

    Try: $n \stackrel{?}{=} 15$

    _____

7. $x - 9 \leq 23$

    Try: $x \stackrel{?}{=} 30$

    _____

8. $\frac{b}{3} > 10$

    Try: $b \stackrel{?}{=} 36$

    _____

9. $25 + w \geq 42$

    Try: $w \stackrel{?}{=} 17$

    _____

10. $9s < 72$

    Try: $s \stackrel{?}{=} 5$

    _____

Write an inequality for each graph. Use *x* for the variable.

11.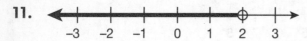

    _____

12.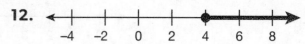

    _____

REMEMBER An open circle means that the point is not in the solution set.

13.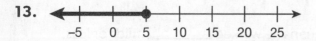

    _____

14.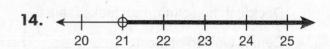

    _____

Solve each inequality. Graph the solution. Use *Math Tool: Blank Number Lines.*

15. $2w > 20$

_____

16. $m - 5 \geq 36$

_____

17. $\frac{y}{6} \leq 9$

_____

18. $x + 23 < 50$

_____

19. $9s \geq 108$

_____

20. $76 + c < 82$

_____

21. $b - 16 > 4$

_____

22. $\frac{h}{5} \leq 25$

_____

Solve.

23. Kareem spent $8 less than Marco spent at the mall. Kareem spent more than $15. How much did Marco spend at the mall?

_____

24. Jamie has 3 times as many pencils as pens. She has at least 18 pencils. How many pens does Jamie have?

_____

25. **DEDUCE** In which direction on the number line do you draw the solution graph of an inequality that has a > or a ≥ symbol? In which direction do you draw the solution graph of an inequality that has a < or a ≤ symbol?

_____

_____

26. **JUSTIFY** How far to the left can you extend the graphs when graphing the solution sets for questions 1 and 3? Explain.

_____

_____

25 Dependent and Independent Variables

An equation such as $y = x - 2$ shows how the variables x and y are related. The value of y depends on the value of x, so x is the **independent variable** and y is the **dependent variable**. The equation shows that whatever the value of x is, the value of y is 2 less than that value. You can use a table of values to show this relationship. Each line of the table can also be expressed as an ordered pair (x, y). So the ordered pairs for this table are (5, 3), (12, 10), and (15, 13).

x	y
5	3
12	10
15	13

EXAMPLE A The table at the right shows the relationship between the weight in pounds on Earth, E, and the weight on Mars, M. The equation $M = 0.38E$ also models the relationship. Which is the independent variable? Which is the dependent variable?

E	M
50	19
100	38
150	57
200	76

1

Use words to express the equation.

Equation: $M = 0.38E$

Verbal expression of the equation:
The weight on Mars equals 0.38 times the weight on Earth.

2

Use the equation to fill in the table.

For each weight on Earth, multiply the weight by 0.38 to find the weight on Mars.

So to fill in the values in the table, select the weight on Earth, then use the equation to find the weight on Mars.

TRY

The table shows the relationship between the weight in pounds on the moon, m, and the weight on Earth, e. The equation $e = 6.02m$ also models the relationship. Which is the independent variable? Which is the dependent variable? Why?

m	e
10	60.2
20	120.4
30	180.6
40	240.8

3

Decide which is the independent variable and which is the dependent variable.

You are choosing an Earth weight and applying the rule to find a Mars weight.

▶ For the equation $M = 0.38E$, E is the independent variable; whatever value you choose for E determines the value of M, the dependent variable.

EXAMPLE B The table shows the relationship between the number of pizzas, n, and the total cost in dollars of the pizzas, c. Write an equation to model the relationship. Which is the independent variable? Which is the dependent variable?

n	c
1	14
2	28
3	42
4	56
5	70

1

Look for a relationship between the variables in the table.

The first row in the table shows that for each pizza bought, the cost is $14.

2

Use the relationship to write an equation.

The total cost in dollars, c, is 14 times the number of pizzas, n.

So $c = 14n$ models the relationship.

3

Decide which is the independent variable and which is the dependent variable.

The total cost depends on the number of pizzas.

The independent variable is the number of pizzas, n.

The dependent variable is the total cost, c.

▶ The equation $c = 14n$ models the relationship. The independent variable is n, and the dependent variable is c.

DISCUSS

How can you verify that the equation works for every value in the table?

EXAMPLE C The graph shows the number of dollars, d, Sariah earns for each hour, h, she works. List the ordered pairs for the points shown on the graph. Which is the independent variable? Which is the dependent variable?

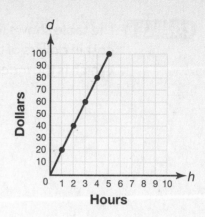

1

List the ordered pair for each point shown on the graph.

The first number in the ordered pair is the number on the horizontal axis, h, that lines up with the point. The second number in the ordered pair is the number on the vertical axis, d, that lines up with the point.

The ordered pairs are (1, 20), (2, 40), (3, 60), (4, 80), and (5, 100).

2

Decide which is the independent variable and which is the dependent variable.

In an ordered pair, the first number represents the independent variable.

The second number represents the dependent variable.

The ordered pairs are in the form (h, d).

The independent variable is h, and the dependent variable is d.

This makes sense because the number of dollars Sariah earns depends on the number of hours she works.

▶ The ordered pairs are (1, 20), (2, 40), (3, 60), (4, 80), and (5, 100). The independent variable is h, and the dependent variable is d.

DISCUSS

How can you use the ordered pairs to write an equation that models the relationship shown by the graph? What is the equation?

⚙ Problem Solving

READ

The graph shows Gavin's age, g, and Celia's age, c. Identify the independent variable and the dependent variable. What equation expresses the relationship of Gavin's age and Celia's age?

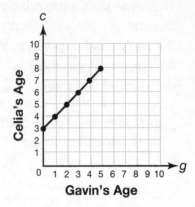

PLAN

List the ordered pairs. Identify the independent variable and the dependent variable.

Relate the value of each c variable to the value of the corresponding g variable.

Write the equation for the relationship between Gavin's and Celia's ages.

SOLVE

When you read an ordered pair on the graph, whose age do you read first? Why?

_____

The ordered pairs are in the form (___, ___) and are (1, 4), (2, 5), (___, ___), (___, ___), (___, ___).

The independent variable is _____. The dependent variable is _____.

How is each c value related to the corresponding g value? c is _____ greater than g.

The equation for the relationship between Gavin's age and Celia's age is _____.

CHECK

Use the graph. How old is Celia when Gavin is 5? _____

Use the equation $c = g + 3$ and substitute 5 for g. _____

Does the equation $c = g + 3$ match the information on the graph? _____

▶ The independent variable is _____. The dependent variable is _____.

The equation is _____.

Practice

1. The table shows the relationship between the age of a plant in months, m, and the height of the plant, h. Which is the independent variable? Which is the dependent variable?

   > **HINT** The height of the plant depends on its age.

m	h
1	8
2	16
3	24
4	32

   _____

   _____

2. The table shows the relationship between the number of quarts, q, and the number of cups, c. Write an equation to model the relationship. Which is the independent variable? Which is the dependent variable?

   > **REMEMBER** For an equation in the form $y = 4 + x$ or $y = 4x$, y is the dependent variable.

q	c
1	4
2	8
3	12
4	16
5	20

   _____

   _____

3. The table shows the relationship between Aubrey's age, A, and Malin's age, M. Which is the independent variable? Which is the dependent variable?

A	M
1	3
2	4
3	5
4	6
5	7

   _____

   _____

4. Evan makes wooden puzzle boxes. The graph shows the number of dollars, *d*, Evan earns for each puzzle box, *b*, he sells. List the ordered pairs shown on the graph. Which is the independent variable? Which is the dependent variable? Write an equation that expresses the relationship between the number of puzzle boxes sold and the amount Evan earns.

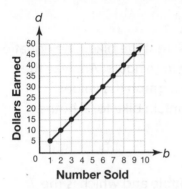

_____

_____

_____

5. The graph shows the distance, *d*, Mr. Benson traveled each hour, *h*, on a trip. List the ordered pairs shown on the graph. Which is the independent variable? Which is the dependent variable? Write an equation that expresses the relationship between the number of miles traveled and the number of hours of travel time.

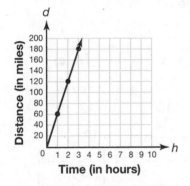

_____

_____

_____

6. **SUMMARIZE** Which axis represents the independent variable on a graph? Which axis represents the dependent variable on a graph? Explain.

_____

_____

7. **ANALYZE** How are an equation, a table of values, a set of ordered pairs, and a graph of the equation related? Does the independent variable change in the representations? Does the dependent variable change in the representations?

_____

_____

LESSON 26 Problem Solving: Using Equations

Mountain Bike Rental

READ

Avery wants to rent a mountain bike. It costs $5 per hour to rent the bike. The equation $c = 5h$ represents the cost, c, of renting the mountain bike for h hours. Analyze the variables. Use the equation to create a table of values. Then graph the values. Use the graph to determine the cost if Avery rents the mountain bike for 7 hours.

PLAN

Analyze the variables. Decide which is the dependent variable and which is the independent variable. Make a table of values for the equation $c = 5h$. Include at least five ordered pairs in the table.

SOLVE

The dependent variable is c, and the independent variable is h.
Use the equation. Complete the table.

h	$c = 5h$	c	(h, c)
1	$c = 5h = 5(1) = 5$	5	$(1, 5)$
2	$c = 5h = 5(2) = $ ____	10	$(2, 10)$
3	$c = 5h = 5(3) = $ ____	____	$(3,$ ___$)$
4	$c = 5h = 5($____$) = $ ____	____	$($___$,$ ___$)$
5	$c = 5h = $ ____ $(5) = $ ____	____	$($___$,$ ___$)$

Plot the ordered pairs on the coordinate plane.
Then connect the points with a straight line.

CHECK

How do you know that your graph is accurate? _____

_____

_____

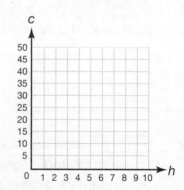

▶ The graph of $c = 5h$ is shown on the right. The cost for

Avery to rent the mountain bike for 7 hours is _____.

Carnival Time

READ

A ticket for each ride at the carnival costs $2. Write an equation to represent the cost, c, of going to the carnival and riding r rides. Analyze the variables. Graph the equation. Use the graph to determine how many rides you could go on if you have $20.

PLAN

Decide which is the dependent variable and which is the independent variable.
Make a table of values.
Use the table of values to write the equation.
Then use the table of values to graph the equation.

SOLVE

The total cost, c, depends on the number of rides, r.

The dependent variable is _____. The independent variable is _____.

Make a table of values.

r	c
1	2
2	_____
3	_____
4	_____
5	_____

Write an equation to represent this situation. _____

Graph the equation. Then connect the points with a straight line.

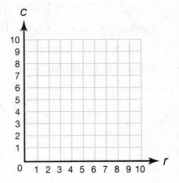

CHECK

How do you know that your graph is accurate?

_____

_____

 An equation to represent the situation is _____. The graph of the equation is shown above. If you have $20, you can go on _____ rides.

Practice

Use the 4-step problem-solving process to solve each problem.

1. **READ** Each box at a market contains 6 oranges. Make a table of values to show the relationship between the number of boxes, b, and the number of oranges, n, that are at the market. Analyze the variables. Write an equation to represent the relationship. Then graph the relationship. Use *Math Tool: Grids* to draw the graph. How many boxes of oranges are in the market if there are 48 oranges?

   PLAN _____

   _____

   SOLVE

   CHECK

2. Diego is 4 years older than May. Write an equation to show the relationship between Diego's age, D, and May's age, M. Make a table of values. Then graph the relationship. Use *Math Tool: Grids* to draw the graph. How old will Diego be when May is 8 years old?

3. Akira earns $8 each day she cares for her neighbor's dog. Write an equation to represent the relationship between the amount of money Akira earns, m, and the number of days, d, that she cares for the dog. Then graph the relationship. Use *Math Tool: Grids* to draw the graph. How much will Akira earn if she cares for the dog for 5 days?

4. Hugo rides his bike at an average rate of 15 miles per hour. Write an equation to represent the relationship between the distance, d, that Hugo rides and the number of hours, h, that he rides. Then graph the relationship. Use *Math Tool: Grids* to draw the graph. How far will Hugo ride if he rides his bike for 3 hours?

5. Every time Luke puts a dime into the parking meter, he gets 10 minutes of parking time. The equation $p = 10d$ represents the time, p, he can park after he puts d dimes into the meter. Analyze the variables. Use the equation to create a table of values. Then graph the values. Use *Math Tool: Grids* to draw the graph. If he puts 5 dimes into the meter, can Luke park for more than or for less than 1 hour?

3 Review

Evaluate each expression.

1. $9^2 - 5^2$

2. $72 - 20 \div 4 + 2^3$

3. $108 \div (2 + 1)^2$

4. $7 \times 5^2 - 4 \times 8$

5. $2^4 \div 4 + 13$

6. $85 - 6^2 \div 3$

Write an algebraic expression for each verbal expression. Let n = the number.

7. 29 more than a number

8. 61 decreased by a number

9. the quotient of 45 and a number

10. subtract 31 from a number

Write a verbal expression for each algebraic expression.

11. $26m$

12. $w - 34$

13. $16 + y$

14. $x \div 8$

Evaluate the algebraic expression for the given value of the variable.

15. $68 - y^2$ for $y = 5$

16. $104 - 6c + 3$ for $c = 1\frac{1}{2}$

17. $30a - 8 \times 3 + 4$ for $a = 4.6$

18. $9.7 + 3.1w - 1.9$ for $w = 2.3$

Choose the best answer.

19. Which expression is equivalent to $d + d + d + d + d$?

   A. $5 + d$ **B.** $5d$

   C. d^5 **D.** $\frac{d}{5}$

20. Which expression is equivalent to $w \times w \times w$?

   A. $w + 3$ **B.** $3w$

   C. w^3 **D.** $\frac{w}{3}$

Write an equivalent expression for each expression.

21. $s + s + s$

22. $p \times p \times p \times p \times p$

23. $x \times x$

24. $n + n + n + n$

Use the distributive property to write an equivalent expression for each expression.

25. $3(y + 5)$

26. $5(4 + 3k)$

27. $7(3n + p)$

28. $10(6w + 2x)$

Write which of the numbers, if any, is a solution of the equation.

29. $35x = 24.5$ Try: 0.7, 0.8, 0.9 _____

30. $2\frac{3}{8} + y = 5\frac{3}{4}$ Try: $3\frac{1}{4}, 3\frac{1}{8}, 3\frac{3}{8}$ _____

Write which numbers, if any, are solutions of the inequality.

31. $n + 9 < 15$ $n \overset{?}{=} 3, 5, 6, 7, 9$ _____

32. $6x > 138$ $x \overset{?}{=} 22, 23, 24, 25$ _____

33. $y - 7 \leq 29$ $y \overset{?}{=} 22, 30, 36, 38$ _____

34. $23 + r \geq 50$ $r \overset{?}{=} 20, 25, 27, 30$ _____

For questions 35–38, write an inequality for each situation.

35. Kendall has at least 20 sports cards. _____

36. Ryder hiked no more than 8 miles. _____

37. Adela saved more than $36. _____

38. Kazuo lost fewer than 9 points. _____

39. Lauren is 6 years older than Erik. Write an equation to show the relationship between Lauren's age, L, and Erik's age, E. Make a table of values. Then graph the relationship. Use *Math Tool: Grids* to draw the graph. How old will Lauren be when Erik is 18 years old?

_____

Solve.

40. Mulan earns $14 per hour. Write and solve an equation to find how many hours she worked if she earned $112.

_____

41. Dennis spent $5 less on lunch than he spent on dinner. Dennis spent at most $12 on dinner. Write and solve an inequality to find how much Dennis spent on lunch.

_____

42. CREATE Write a word problem that can be solved by the equation $108 \div r = 12$.

_____

43. REWRITE Refer to question 41 and suppose that Dennis spends *at least* $12 on dinner. Modify the equation and your solution to fit the new problem.

_____

Some **Weighty** Questions

In the balance-scale puzzles shown here, the value of *x* will not be a number. Instead, it will be one or more shapes.

Example: The two scales below are both in balance. What shape or shapes does *x* represent?

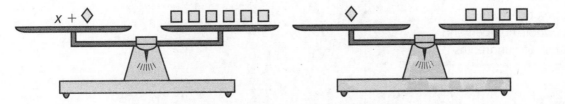

In this puzzle, *x* + 1 diamond are balanced by 6 squares and 1 diamond is balanced by 4 squares.

To find the shape(s) represented by *x*, you can remove the diamond from the left side of the first scale. To keep the first scale in balance, you also need to remove the equivalent of 1 diamond from the right side of the scale. The second scale shows that the equivalent of 1 diamond is 4 squares. When you remove 1 diamond from the left and 4 squares from the right, then *x* will be by itself on the left side of the first scale. It will be balanced by 2 squares. So in this puzzle, *x* represents 2 squares.

Now try the puzzle below on your own, with a partner, or with a small group. (Beware! This puzzle is not as easy as the one shown above.)

The three scales below are all in balance. What shape or shapes does *x* represent? Explain your solution.

Scale 1:

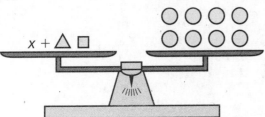

Scale 2:

Scale 3:

Grade 5 NBT

Perform operations with multi-digit whole numbers and with decimals to hundredths.

Grade 5 NF

Apply and extend previous understandings of multiplication and division to multiply and divide fractions.

Grade 5 MD

Geometric measurement: understand concepts of volume and relate volume to multiplication and to addition.

Grade 6 G

Solve real-world and mathematical problems involving area, surface area, and volume.

Grade 7 G

Draw, construct, and describe geometrical figures and describe the relationships between them.

Solve real-life and mathematical problems involving angle measure, area, surface area, and volume.

Grade 5 G

Graph points on the coordinate plane to solve real-world and mathematical problems.

Classify two-dimensional figures into categories based on their properties.

Domain 4
Geometry

Finding the Area of Triangles and Quadrilaterals

LESSON 27

UNDERSTAND **Area** is the number of square units (units²) in the interior of a figure.

Find the area of the **quadrilateral**.

1

The quadrilateral is a **parallelogram**.
Count the number of whole squares inside.
Count the number of partial squares inside.

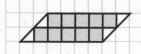

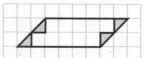

There are 10 whole squares.

Each partial square is $\frac{1}{2}$ of a whole square.
There are 4 halves. This is the same as 2 whole squares.

2

Add the number of whole and partial squares to find the area.
10 + 2 = 12
The area of the parallelogram is 12 square units.

3

Relate the area of the parallelogram to the area of a rectangle having the same length and width as the base and height of the parallelogram. Draw the height of the parallelogram from one corner of the parallelogram to its base. This forms a **right triangle**. Notice that you can make a right triangle with the same area by drawing the height outside the **triangle** and extending the base. Both triangles have a height of 2 units and a base of 2 units.

The area of the rectangle is 6 × 2, or 12, square units.
The area of the parallelogram is 12 square units.

The models show that the area of a parallelogram with base b and height h is the same as the area of a rectangle with base b and height h.

▶ The area of the parallelogram is 12 square units.

← Connect

Find the area of the parallelogram.

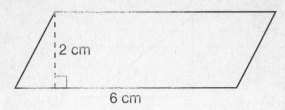

2 cm

6 cm

1

Write the formula for the area of a parallelogram.

$A = bh$

2

Identify the base and the height of the parallelogram.

The base is 6 cm.

The height forms a right angle with the base. The height is 2 cm.

3

Find the area.

$A = bh$

$A = 6\ cm \times 2\ cm$ ← Substitute 6 for b and 2 for h in the formula.

$A = 12\ cm^2$ ← Simplify.

▶ The area of the parallelogram is $12\ cm^2$.

DISCUSS

Why do you include cm^2 in the answer for the area of the parallelogram?

EXAMPLE A Find the area of the right triangle.

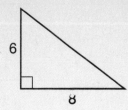

1 Write the formula for the area of a triangle.

$A = \frac{1}{2}bh$

2 Identify the base and the height of the triangle.

The base is 8 units.

The height is 6 units.

3 Find the area.

$A = \frac{1}{2}bh$

$A = \frac{1}{2} \times 8 \times 6$ ← Substitute 8 for b and 6 for h in the formula.

$A = 24$ units^2 ← Simplify.

4 Find the area of the triangle by decomposing a rectangle.

Draw a horizontal line from the top of the triangle and a vertical line from the end of the base to create a rectangle.

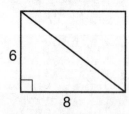

The area of the rectangle is 6×8, or 48, units^2.

The area of the triangle is half the area of the rectangle: $\frac{1}{2} \times 48$ units^2 or 24 units^2.

▶ The area of the triangle is 24 units^2.

DISCUSS

Why is it true that the area of the triangle that resulted from decomposing the rectangle is half the area of the rectangle?

EXAMPLE B Find the area of the triangle.

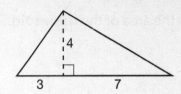

1 Identify the base and the height of the triangle.

The base is 3 + 7, or 10, units.

The height forms a right angle with the base. The height is 4 units.

2 Write the formula for the area of a triangle to find the area.

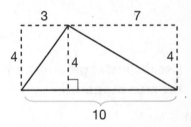

$A = \frac{1}{2}bh$

$A = \frac{1}{2} \times 10 \times 4$ ← Substitute 10 for b and 4 for h in the formula.

$A = 20$ unit^2 ← Simplify.

3 Find the area of the triangle by decomposing a rectangle.

Create a rectangle by using the base of the triangle as its length and the height of the triangle as its width.

The area of the rectangle is 4 × 10, or 40, units^2.

The area of the triangle to the left of the height line is half the area of the rectangle with length 3 and width 4:

$\frac{1}{2} \times 3 \times 4$ or 6 units^2.

The area of the triangle to the right of the height line is half the area of the rectangle with length 7 and width 4:

$\frac{1}{2} \times 7 \times 4$ or 14 units^2.

So the area of the decomposed triangle is 6 + 14, or 20, units^2.

▶ The area of the triangle is 20 units^2.

MODEL

Find the area of the triangle by decomposing a rectangle.

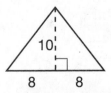

EXAMPLE C Find the area of the **trapezoid**.

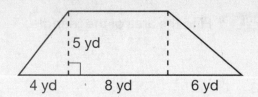

5 yd

4 yd · 8 yd · 6 yd

1

Find familiar figures that make up the trapezoid.

The trapezoid is composed of two triangles and a rectangle.

Label the left triangle "I," the middle rectangle "II," and the right triangle "III."

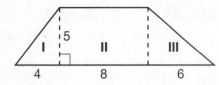

5

I · II · III

4 · 8 · 6

2

Use the triangle area formula to find the area of figure I.

$A = \frac{1}{2}bh$

$A = \frac{1}{2} \times 4 \text{ yd} \times 5 \text{ yd}$ ← Substitute 4 yd for *b* and 5 yd for *h* in the formula.

$A = 10 \text{ yd}^2$ ← Simplify.

3

Use the rectangle area formula to find the area of figure II.

$A = lw$

$A = 8 \text{ yd} \times 5 \text{ yd}$ ← Substitute 8 yd for *l* and 5 yd for *w* in the formula.

$A = 40 \text{ yd}^2$ ← Simplify.

4

Use the triangle area formula to find the area of figure III.

$A = \frac{1}{2}bh$

$A = \frac{1}{2} \times 6 \text{ yd} \times 5 \text{ yd}$ ← Substitute 6 yd for *b* and 5 yd for *h* in the formula.

$A = 15 \text{ yd}^2$ ← Simplify.

5

Add to find the total area.

A = area of figure I + area of figure II + area of figure III

$A = 10 \text{ yd}^2 + 40 \text{ yd}^2 + 15 \text{ yd}^2$

$A = 65 \text{ yd}^2$ ← Simplify.

▶ The area of the trapezoid is 65 yd^2.

TRY

Suppose the height of the trapezoid above is changed to 3 yards. What is the area of the new trapezoid?

⚙️ Problem Solving

Erik drew the diagram to the right of his irregularly shaped garden to find its total area. What is the area of Erik's garden?

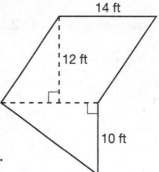

14 ft

12 ft

10 ft

PLAN

Find familiar figures that make up the garden.
Find the area of each figure. Add the areas to find the total area.

SOLVE

The top part of the garden diagram is shaped like a parallelogram.

The base is _____ ft, and the height is _____ ft.

The bottom part of the garden diagram is shaped like a triangle.

The base is _____ ft, and the height is _____ ft.

Use the formula for the area of a _____ to find the area of the top part.

$A =$ _____

$A =$ _____ × _____ ← Substitute values for b and h.

$A =$ _____ ft^2 ← Simplify.

Use the formula for the area of a _____ to find the area of the bottom part.

$A =$ _____

$A =$ _____ × _____ × _____ ← Substitute values for b and h.

$A =$ _____ ft^2 ← Simplify.

Find the total area of the garden.

_____ + _____ = _____

CHECK

Look back at the garden diagram.
Estimate the total area of the garden. _____

Does your answer seem reasonable? Explain _____.

▶ The area of Erik's garden is _____.

Practice

Find the area of each figure.

1. parallelogram

$b = 25$ cm

$h = 18$ cm

_____

2. rectangle

$l = 2\frac{2}{3}$ ft

$w = 1\frac{1}{2}$ ft

_____

3. triangle

$b = 12$ m

$h = 9$ m

_____

4. square

$s = 4.6$ mi

_____

> **HINT** A square is a special parallelogram with sides length s.

Find the area of each figure.

5.

15 in. 26 in.

_____

6.

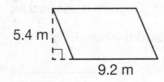

5.4 m

9.2 m

_____

7.

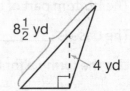

$8\frac{1}{2}$ yd   4 yd

_____

> **REMEMBER** The height forms a right angle with the base.

8.

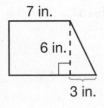

7 in.

6 in.

3 in.

_____

9.

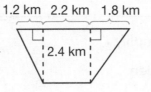

1.2 km   2.2 km   1.8 km

2.4 km

_____

10.

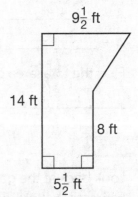

$9\frac{1}{2}$ ft

14 ft

8 ft

$5\frac{1}{2}$ ft

_____

Solve.

11. A rectangular blanket has an area of 24 square feet. The blanket is 6 feet long. How wide is the blanket?

_____

12. A triangular sail has a base of 3 feet and a height of $5\frac{1}{2}$ feet. What is the area of the sail?

_____

13. The area of a square window is 81 square inches. How long is each side of the window?

_____

14. Andrea's garden is shaped like a parallelogram with a base length of 6.5 meters and a height of 4.8 meters. She wants to increase the area by doubling the base length and increasing the height by 1.5 meters. By how much will the changes increase the area of the garden? Explain.

_____

15. A square poster board has sides that are 40 inches long. When the triangular flaps at the sides are opened, the poster board takes the shape of a trapezoid. The base of each triangle is 24 inches. What is the area of the trapezoid poster board?

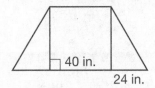

_____

16. A rectangular table is 2.4 meters long and 1.5 meters wide. The table has triangular flaps that can be raised on opposite sides. The base of each flap is 1.2 meters. What is the area of the table when both flaps are raised?

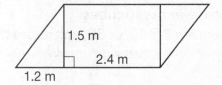

_____

17. **CONSTRUCT** A banner is shaped like a parallelogram. The banner has a base length of 3.25 meters and an area of 4.55 square meters. Explain how to find the height of the banner.

_____

_____

_____

18. **WRITE MATH** Explain how the area of a parallelogram is related to the area of a triangle when both figures have the same base and height.

_____

_____

_____

LESSON 28
Finding the Volume of Rectangular Prisms

UNDERSTAND **Volume** is the number of cubic units needed to fill the space in a three-dimensional figure. Volume is measured in cubic units (units³).

Find the volume of the **rectangular prism**.

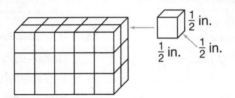

$\frac{1}{2}$ in.

$\frac{1}{2}$ in. $\frac{1}{2}$ in.

1

Count the number of cubes in the top layer of the prism.

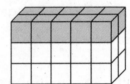

There are 10 cubes in the top layer.

2

Find the total number of cubes that fill the prism.
There are 3 layers of cubes that fill the prism.
Each layer has 10 cubes.
There are 3 × 10, or 30, unit cubes that fill the prism.

3

Find the volume of one unit cube.

Each unit cube is $\frac{1}{2}$ inch by $\frac{1}{2}$ inch by $\frac{1}{2}$ inch.

The volume of one unit cube is $\frac{1}{2}$ inch × $\frac{1}{2}$ inch × $\frac{1}{2}$ inch, or $\frac{1}{8}$ cubic inch.

4

Find the volume of the rectangular prism in cubic inches.
Multiply the number of cubic inches in one unit cube by the number of unit cubes that fill the prism.

$\frac{1}{8} \times 30 = \frac{30}{8} = 3\frac{6}{8} = 3\frac{3}{4}$

▶ The volume of the rectangular prism is $3\frac{3}{4}$ cubic inches.

⊂ Connect

Find the volume of the rectangular prism.

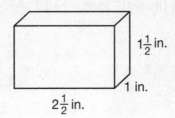

$1\frac{1}{2}$ in.

1 in.

$2\frac{1}{2}$ in.

1 Write the formula for the volume of a rectangular prism.

$V = lwh$, where l = length, w = width, and h = height

2 Identify the length, width, and the height of the rectangular prism.

The length is $2\frac{1}{2}$ inches.

The width is 1 inch.

The height is $1\frac{1}{2}$ inches.

3 Find the volume.

$V = lwh$

$V = 2\frac{1}{2}$ in. $\times$ 1 in. $\times$ $1\frac{1}{2}$ in. ← Substitute $2\frac{1}{2}$ for l, 1 for w, and $1\frac{1}{2}$ for h in the formula.

$= \frac{5}{2}$ in. $\times \frac{1}{1}$ in. $\times \frac{3}{2}$ in. ← Write improper fractions for the mixed numbers.

$= \frac{15}{4}$ in.^{3} ← Multiply.

$= 3\frac{3}{4}$ in.^{3} ← Simplify.

▶ The volume of the rectangular prism is $3\frac{3}{4}$ in.^{3}

TRY

What is the volume of a rectangular prism that is $\frac{2}{3}$ yard long, $\frac{1}{4}$ yard wide, and $1\frac{1}{2}$ yards tall?

EXAMPLE A Find the volume of the rectangular prism that has a length (l) of $5\frac{1}{3}$ feet, a width (w) of $2\frac{1}{2}$ feet, and a height (h) of $8\frac{2}{3}$ feet.

1

Write the formula for the volume of a rectangular prism.

$V = lwh$

2

Find the volume.

$V = lwh$

$= 5\frac{1}{3}$ ft $\times 2\frac{1}{2}$ ft $\times 8\frac{2}{3}$ ft. ← Substitute the values for l, w, and h in the formula.

$= \frac{16}{3}$ ft $\times \frac{5}{2}$ ft $\times \frac{26}{3}$ ft ← Write improper fractions for the mixed numbers.

$= \frac{2080}{18}$ ft^3 ← Multiply.

$= \frac{1040}{9}$ ft^3 ← Simplify.

$= 115\frac{5}{9}$ ft^3

▶ The volume of the rectangular prism is $115\frac{5}{9}$ ft^3.

EXAMPLE B What is the height of a box that has the shape of a rectangular prism, if the volume is 105 cubic inches and the area of the base is 30 square inches?

1

Use the formula for the volume of a rectangular prism.

The area of the base is known, so substitute B for lw in the formula.

$V = Bh$

2

Find the height.

$V = Bh$ ← Substitute known values for V and B.

$105 = 30h$

$\frac{105}{30} = \frac{30h}{30}$ ← Divide both sides by 30.

$3\frac{1}{2} = h$

▶ So $h = 3\frac{1}{2}$ inches. The height of the box is $3\frac{1}{2}$ inches.

TRY

What is the height of a rectangular prism that has a volume of $10\frac{1}{2}$ cubic yards if its base is $2\frac{1}{4}$ yards long and $1\frac{1}{3}$ yards wide?

⚙️ Problem Solving

A gift box shown at the right is packed with small cubic $\frac{1}{2}$ inch blocks. The blocks are packed tightly with no spaces between. How many blocks are in the gift box? What is the volume of the box in cubic inches?

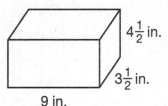

4½ in.

3½ in.

9 in.

PLAN

Find how many $\frac{1}{2}$ inch lengths are equivalent to the length, width, and height.

Multiply the products to find the total number of blocks.

Use the formula for the volume of a _____.

SOLVE

The length is _____ inches, so the box is 2 × _____, or _____ blocks long.

The width is _____ inches, so the box is 2 × _____, or _____ blocks wide.

The height is _____ inches, so the box is 2 × _____, or _____ blocks high.

So the total number of blocks = 18 × 7 × _____ = _____.

Use the formula to find the volume.

$V = $ _____

$V = $ _____ × _____ × _____   ← Substitute values for l, w, and h.

$V = $ _____ × _____ × _____   ← Change to improper fractions.

$V = $ _____ in.^{3} ← Multiply.

$V = $ _____ in.^{3} ← Simplify.

CHECK

The volume of each block is $\frac{1}{2}$ inch × $\frac{1}{2}$ inch × $\frac{1}{2}$ inch, or _____ in.^{3}

Is the total number of blocks times the volume of each block equal to the volume of the box in cubic inches? _____

▶ The number of blocks in the box is _____. The volume of the box is _____ in.^{3}

Practice

Find the volume of each figure.

1.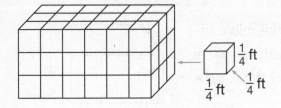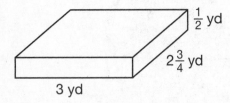

HINT Find the volume of each unit cube.

_____

2.

$\frac{1}{2}$ yd

$2\frac{3}{4}$ yd

3 yd

3.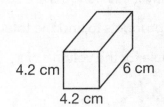

4.2 cm   6 cm

4.2 cm

_____   _____

Find the volume of each rectangular prism.

4. $l = 24$ cm, $w = 18$ cm, $h = 1.6$ cm

5. $B = 316$ m^2, $h = 58$ m

_____

REMEMBER You can use the area of the base to find the volume of a prism.

6. $l = 3.5$ m, $w = 8$ m, $h = 2.25$ m

7. $l = 9$ in., $w = 4\frac{1}{2}$ in., $h = 5$ in.

_____   _____

8. $B = 2\frac{2}{3}$ yd^2, $h = 1\frac{1}{2}$ yd

9. $l = 4\frac{2}{3}$ ft, $w = 2$ ft, $h = \frac{1}{3}$ ft

_____   _____

10. $l = 15$ in., $w = 6\frac{3}{8}$ in., $h = 4\frac{1}{2}$ in.

11. $B = 6\frac{1}{2}$ ft^2, $h = 2\frac{3}{4}$ ft

_____   _____

Find the missing dimension of each rectangular prism.

12. $l = 14$ cm, $w = ?$, $h = 3$ cm, $V = 294$ cm^3 _____

13. $B = 48$ in.^{2}, $h = ?$, $V = 576$ in.^{3} _____

14. $l = ?$, $w = \frac{3}{4}$ ft, $h = 4$ ft, $V = 4\frac{1}{2}$ ft^3 _____

15. $l = 1$ in., $w = 3\frac{1}{2}$ in., $h = ?$, $V = 18\frac{3}{8}$ in.^{3} _____

16. $B = ?$, $h = 8\frac{1}{2}$ yd, $V = 76\frac{1}{2}$ yd^3 _____

Solve.

17. A cereal box is $6\frac{1}{2}$ inches long, $4\frac{1}{4}$ inches wide, and 10 inches tall. What is the volume of the cereal box?

    _____

18. A display case is shaped like a cube. Each side of the display case is $8\frac{1}{2}$ inches long. What is the volume of the display case?

    _____

19. The floor of a rectangular storage bin has an area of 72 square feet. The volume of the bin is 270 cubic feet. How tall is the storage bin?

    _____

20. An aquarium has a volume of 9,525 cm^3. The aquarium is 12.5 centimeters wide and 30 centimeters tall. How long is the aquarium?

    _____

21. **ANALYZE** Explain why area is measured in square units and volume is measured in cubic units.

    _____

    _____

22. **DEMONSTRATE** Draw a rectangular prism. Select lengths for the length, width, and height. Label the dimensions. Explain how to find the volume of the prism using the two formulas for volume.

    _____

    _____

    _____

29 Drawing Polygons on the Coordinate Plane

EXAMPLE A Plot the given points, and connect them in order to form a polygon.

$A(-4, -3); B(-2, 2); C(2, 2); D(4, -3); E(0, -5)$

Then use coordinates to find the number of units from one point to another for two points that lie on the same horizontal line.

1

Plot each point.

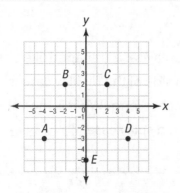

2

Connect the points in the order they were given. Then connect the first and last points.

Draw 5 line segments to form a polygon.

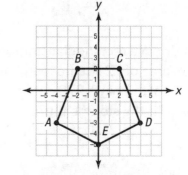

3

Look at line segment *BC*.

The coordinates for point *B* are $(-2, 2)$, and the coordinates for point *C* are $(2, 2)$.

Since line segment *BC* is horizontal, both points have the same *y*-coordinate.

Use the *x*-coordinates to find the number of units from either point to the other.

4

Find the absolute value of the difference of the *x*-coordinates.

$|-2 - 2| = |-4| = 4$

▶ Points *B* and *C* lie on the same horizontal line. The number of units from point *B* to point *C* is 4.

TRY

How many units are there from point *P* at $(-5, 4)$ to point *Q* at $(8, 4)$?

Use coordinates. Then check by plotting the points and counting units.

You can use *Math Tool: Coordinate Grid* to plot the points.

EXAMPLE B Plot the given points, and connect them in order to form a polygon.

$F(3, 4); G(3, -3); H(-1, -5); J(-5, -3); K(-5, 4)$

Then use coordinates to find the number of units from one point to another for two points that lie on the same vertical line.

1

Plot each point.

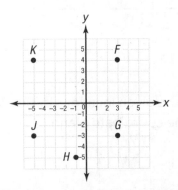

2

Connect the points in the order they were given. Then connect the first and last points.

Draw 5 line segments to form a polygon.

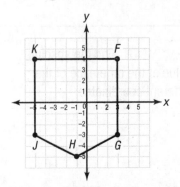

3

Look at line segment *JK*.

The coordinates for point *J* are $(-5, -3)$, and the coordinates for point *K* are $(-5, 4)$.

Since line segment *JK* is vertical, both points have the same *x*-coordinate.

Use the *y*-coordinates to find the number of units from either point to the other.

4

Find the absolute value of the difference of the *y*-coordinates.

$|-3 - 4| = |-7| = 7$

▶ Points *J* and *K* lie on **the same** vertical line. The number of **units** from point *J* to point *K* is 7.

TRY

How many units are there from point *R* at $(-5, -7)$ to point *S* at $(-5, 9)$?

Use coordinates. Then check by plotting the points and counting units.

You can use *Math Tool: Coordinate Grid* to plot the points.

Practice

Use the information given below for questions 1–3.

The center of Tiny Town could be laid out on a coordinate plane with each unit representing one block. The bank would be located at $(-2, 3)$, the stadium at $(2, 3)$, the grocery store at $(-2, -1)$, and the movie theater at $(2, -4)$.

1. Which two places in Tiny Town lie on the same horizontal line? How do you know?

    _____

     Look for ordered pairs with the same *y*-coordinate.

2. How many blocks is it from the bank to the grocery store?

    _____

    REMEMBER Find the absolute value of the difference of the different coordinates.

3. Plot the given locations in Tiny Town on the coordinate plane.

    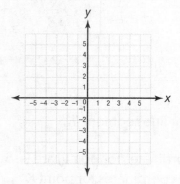

Use the information given below for questions 4–8.

The coordinates of the vertices of trapezoid *JKLM* are *J*(4, 1), *K*(2, −3), *L* (−4, −3), and *M*(−4, 1).

4. Which sides of the trapezoid are horizontal line segments? _____

5. How many units long is the vertical line? _____

6. How many units long is side *KL*? _____

7. How many units long is side *MJ*? _____

8. Using a grid from *Math Tool: Coordinate Planes*, plot the points to form trapezoid *JKLM*.

Use the information given below for questions 9–15.

The stations for different points of interest along a scenic drive in a state park could be laid out on a coordinate plane with each unit representing one mile. The following shows the coordinates of each station.

Station A: $(-5, 4)$ Station B: $(-2, 4)$ Station C: $(-2, 5)$ Station D: $(5, 5)$

Station E: $(5, -2)$ Station F: $(2, -2)$ Station G: $(2, -4)$

Station H: $(-1, -4)$ Station I: $(-1, 1)$ Station J: $(-5, 1)$

Find the distance between the stations. Indicate whether the line along which the stations lie is horizontal or vertical.

9.   Station A to Station B _____

10. Station B to Station C _____

11. Station E to Station F _____

12. Station F to Station G _____

13. Station I to Station J _____

14. Station J back to Station A _____

15. Using a grid from *Math Tool: Coordinate Planes*, plot and label the stations in order. Draw the polygon formed when the stations are connected.

Solve.

16. EXPLAIN Refer back to the information given for questions 4–8. Can you use the methods presented in this lesson to find the length of side *JK*? Explain why or why not.

_____

_____

_____

17. DESCRIBE Describe the procedure you would follow to find the length of each side of the rectangle formed when points $(-4, 5)$, $(4, 5)$, $(4, -4)$, and $(-4, -4)$ are connected.

_____

_____

_____

30 Representing Three-Dimensional Figures Using Nets

A **three-dimensional figure** that has two congruent, parallel, triangular **bases** and three rectangular sides is a **triangular prism**. A **net** is a flat pattern that can be folded to form a three-dimensional figure.

EXAMPLE A The figure on the right is the net of a three-dimensional figure. If the net were folded along the dashed lines, what three-dimensional figure would it form?

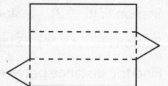

1

Identify the shapes that make up the net.

Each **two-dimensional figure** on the net represents one **face** of the three-dimensional figure. The net is made from 3 rectangles and 2 triangles.

So 3 faces of the three-dimensional figure are rectangles and 2 faces are triangles.

2

Create the figure.

The net can be folded along the dashed lines.

Think of folding the rectangular faces up along the longer dashed lines first.
The top and bottom rectangles will meet along the two long, solid lines.
Then the triangles on the ends can be folded to close up the figure.
The three-dimensional figure formed is shown below.

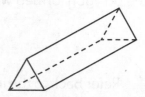

DISCUSS

If the triangles were on opposite sides of the middle rectangle, would the net still be able to be folded into a triangular prism? What if the triangles were on opposite sides of the top rectangle? Trace, modify, and cut out to experiment with different nets. Is there only one correct net for a three-dimensional figure, or could there be more than one?

3

The three-dimensional figure has 3 rectangular faces and 2 triangular faces.

The 2 triangular faces are parallel.

▶ The three-dimensional figure represented by the net is a triangular prism.

A pyramid has a single base and has triangular faces that all meet at the same point. A pyramid is named by the shape of its base.

EXAMPLE B Draw the net of the **rectangular pyramid** shown below.

1

Identify the shape of each face.

The base, or bottom face, of the pyramid is a rectangle.

Each side face of the pyramid is a triangle.

There are 4 triangular faces.

2

Draw the net.

First draw a rectangle to represent the base.

Used dashed lines to represent the base.

Then draw triangles along each side of the rectangle to represent the triangular faces.

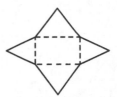

If the triangles were folded up along the dashed lines and slanted so they all met at one point, a rectangular pyramid would be formed.

▶ The net above is a net of the rectangular pyramid.

CHECK

How can you check that your net represents the three-dimensional figure?

Practice

What three-dimensional figure does each net represent?

1.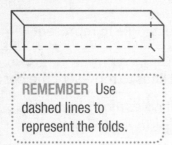

   _____

2.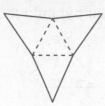

   _____

   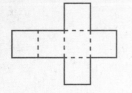
   HINT A pyramid is named by the shape of its base.

3.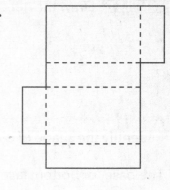

   _____

Draw a net for each three-dimensional figure.

4.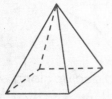

   REMEMBER Use dashed lines to represent the folds.

5.

6.

Solve.

7. Viola folded the net shown to create a three-dimensional figure. What figure did she make?

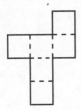

_____

8. Mason drew the nets shown to represent two different three-dimensional figures. How are the figures similar? How are they different? What are the figures?

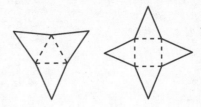

_____

9. A tent is shaped like the three-dimensional figure shown. What three-dimensional figure is the tent? Draw a net of the tent.

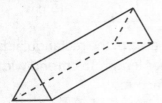

10. A cereal box is shaped like the three-dimensional figure shown. What three-dimensional figure is the box? Draw a net of the cereal box.

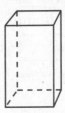

11. **DESCRIBE** How do you use a net to determine the three-dimensional figure it represents?

_____

_____

_____

12. **WRITE MATH** Explain how to draw the net of a three-dimensional figure.

_____

_____

_____

31 Using Nets to Find Surface Area

EXAMPLE What is the surface area of the triangular prism?

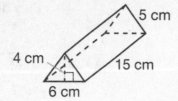

1

Draw a net of the triangular prism.

Draw the net.

Label the lengths of the sides.

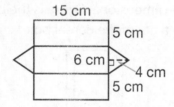

2

Use the net to find the area of each face of the triangular prism.

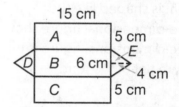

Find the area of the rectangular faces.
Face A has length 15 cm and width 5 cm.
Area of face A:
$A = lw = 15 \text{ cm} \times 5 \text{ cm} = 75 \text{ cm}^2$

Face B has length 15 cm and width 6 cm.
Area of face B:
$A = lw = 15 \text{ cm} \times 6 \text{ cm} = 90 \text{ cm}^2$

Face C has length 15 cm and width 5 cm.
Face C has the same area as face A.

Find the area of the triangular faces.
Face D has base 6 cm and height 4 cm.
Area of face D: $A = \frac{1}{2}bh$
$= \frac{1}{2} \times 6 \text{ cm} \times 4 \text{ cm} = 12 \text{ cm}^2$
Face E has the same area as face D.

3

Find the surface area of the triangular prism.

To find the **surface area**, add the areas of the all the faces of the triangular prism.
$SA = 75 \text{ cm}^2 + 90 \text{ cm}^2 + 75 \text{ cm}^2 +$
$\quad 12 \text{ cm}^2 + 12 \text{ cm}^2$
$SA = 264 \text{ cm}^2$

▶ The surface area of the triangular prism is 264 cm².

Why do you need only the areas of faces A, B, and D to find the surface area of the triangular prism?

Problem Solving

READ

Raymond has a cereal box that he is planning to paint for a project.
The dimensions of the box are shown to the right. What is the
surface area that he will paint?

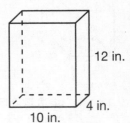

12 in.

4 in.

10 in.

PLAN

Draw a net of the cereal box.

The box is shaped like a _____.

Label the sides of the net that correspond to the cereal box.

Use the net to find the _____ of each face.

Then add the areas to find the _____.

SOLVE

Draw the net, and label the sides.

Each face of the box is a _____.

Use the formula _____ to find the
area of each face.

Find the area of each of the six faces
of the box.

Face 1: _____   Face 2: _____

Face 3: _____   Face 4: _____

Face 5: _____   Face 6: _____

10 in.

4 in.

12 in.

12 in.

4 in.

10 in.

Add to find the total surface area.

_____ + _____ + _____ + _____ + _____ + _____ = _____

CHECK

Does your answer seem reasonable? Explain.

_____

_____

▶ Raymond has to paint a surface area of _____ in.^{2}.

Practice

Draw a net to find the surface area of each three-dimensional figure.

1.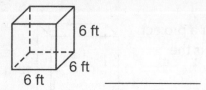

6 ft
6 ft
6 ft

_____

HINT Each face is a square.

2.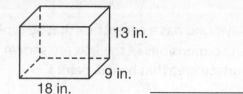

13 in.
9 in.
18 in.

_____

3.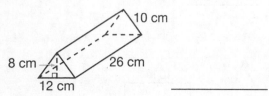

10 cm
8 cm
26 cm
12 cm

_____

REMEMBER Only two of the three rectangular faces are congruent.

4.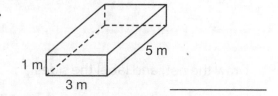

5 m
1 m
3 m

_____

5.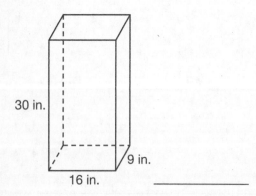

30 in.
9 in.
16 in.

_____

6.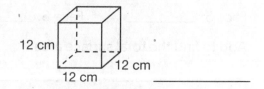

12 cm
12 cm
12 cm

_____

Solve.

7. The dimensions of Femi's tent are shown to the right. Draw a net and use it to find the surface area of her tent.

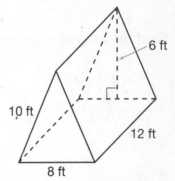

6 ft

10 ft

12 ft

8 ft

_____

8. Elaine's room is in the shape of a rectangular prism 15 feet long, 12 feet wide, and 10 feet tall. Elaine paints the four walls and the ceiling but not the floor. How much surface area does Elaine paint?

_____

9. A Plexiglas display case is shaped like the triangular prism to the right. What is the surface area of the prism?

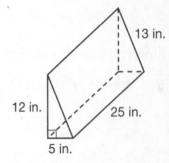

13 in.

12 in.

25 in.

5 in.

_____

10. DEMONSTRATE The net for a rectangular prism is shown to the right. Use the net to find the surface area of the rectangular prism. Show your work.

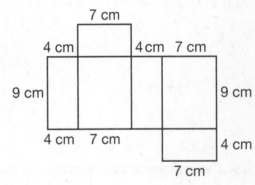

7 cm

4 cm   4 cm   7 cm

9 cm   9 cm

4 cm   7 cm   4 cm

7 cm

11. CLASSIFY What are the similarities and differences for a rectangular pyramid and a triangular prism? How do the nets of these figures help you identify them?

_____

_____

_____

4 Review

Find the area of each figure.

1.
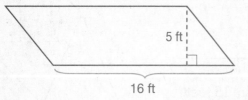
5 ft
16 ft

_____

2.

9 m
12 m

_____

3.

13 cm
15 cm
8 cm

_____

4.
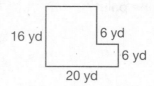
16 yd
6 yd
6 yd
20 yd

_____

Find the volume of each rectangular prism.

5. $B = 78 \text{ ft}^2, h = 23 \text{ ft}$

_____

6. $l = 4.2 \text{ cm}, w = 3.8 \text{ cm}, h = 6 \text{ cm}$

_____

7. $l = 8\frac{3}{4} \text{ in.}, w = 9 \text{ in.}, h = 15 \text{ in.}$

_____

8. $B = 4\frac{1}{2} \text{ yd}^2, h = 7 \text{ yd}$

_____

9. $l = 6\frac{1}{2} \text{ ft}, w = 5 \text{ ft}, h = 4\frac{1}{4} \text{ ft}$

_____

10. $l = 28 \text{ in.}, w = 18 \text{ in.}, h = 15\frac{1}{2} \text{ in.}$

_____

Use the following information for questions 11–14.

The coordinates of the vertices of pentagon *CDEFG* are *C*(−5, 5), *D*(1, 5), *E*(1, −3), *F*(−3, −4) and *G*(−5, −2).

11. How long is side *CD*?

_____

12. How long is side *DE*?

_____

13. How long is side *CG*?

_____

14. Use a grid from *Math Tool: Coordinate Planes* to plot the points. Draw the polygon formed when the points are connected.

Draw a net for each three-dimensional figure.

15.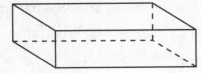

16.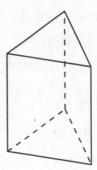

Draw a net to find the surface area of each three-dimensional figure.

17.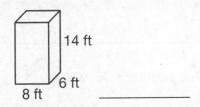

14 ft

6 ft

8 ft

_____

18.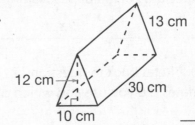

13 cm

12 cm

30 cm

10 cm

_____

Choose the best answer.

19. A rectangular card has an area of $120\frac{1}{4}$ square inches. The card is $6\frac{1}{2}$ inches wide. How long is the card?

   A. $18\frac{1}{4}$ in.   **B.** $18\frac{1}{2}$ in.

   C. $20\frac{1}{4}$ in.   **D.** $781\frac{5}{8}$ in.

20. A block in the shape of a cube has sides that are $2\frac{1}{2}$ inches long. What is the volume of the block?

   A. $8\frac{1}{8}$ in.^{3} **B.** $8\frac{1}{2}$ in.^{3}

   C. 15 in.^{3} **D.** $15\frac{5}{8}$ in.^{3}

Solve.

21. The top of a shoe box has an area of 88 square inches. The volume of the shoe box is 396 cubic inches. How tall is the shoe box?

_____

22. A paperweight shaped like a cube has sides that are 8 centimeters long. Draw a net to find the surface area of the paper weight.

_____

23. (EXPLAIN) Refer back to question 12. To find the length of line segment *DE*, which coordinates did you use and which did you ignore? Why?

_____

_____

24. (DEMONSTRATE) How can you decompose this figure into rectangles and use them to find the area of the polygon?

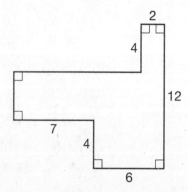

_____

_____

Explore a Prism

1. Choose a rectangular prism in your classroom. Examples include books and boxes of different sizes. Object chosen: _____

2. Measure the length, width, and height of the prism.

    $l =$ _____ $w =$ _____ $h =$ _____

3. Draw the rectangular prism. Label the sides of your drawing using your measurements.

4. Find the volume of the rectangular prism. _____

5. Draw a net of the rectangular prism. Label the side lengths on the net.

6. Find the surface area of the rectangular prism. _____

7. Make a copy of your net, and exchange it with a classmate. Find the surface area of your partner's rectangular prism. Draw your partner's rectangular prism, and label its dimensions. Find the volume of your partner's rectangular prism. Compare answers with your partner.

Grade 5 MD

Represent and interpret data.

Grade 6 SP

Develop understanding of statistical variability.

Summarize and describe distributions.

Grade 7 SP

Use random sampling to draw inferences about a population.

Draw informal comparative inferences about two populations.

Domain 5
Statistics and Probability

LESSON 32 Understanding Statistical Variability

EXAMPLE A Jamal wants to gather statistical information about a math test. He has a list of four questions that he can ask about the math test. Which of the following questions is a statistical question?

1. What grade did Aiden get on his math test?
2. What grade did Tani get on her math test?
3. Who got a higher grade on the math test, Aiden or Tani?
4. What grades did the students in the math class get on their tests?

1 Understand what kind of answer a statistical question involves.

Since Jamal is looking for statistical data, he should ask a question that will result in multiple and varying answers rather than a single answer.

2 Examine each question for variability.

1. What grade did Aiden get on his math test?

This question has one answer, the grade that Aiden got on the test.

2. What grade did Tani get on her math test?

This question also has one answer, the grade that Tani got on the test.

3. Who got a higher grade on the math test, Aiden or Tani?

This question has one answer, whoever got the higher grade on the test.

4. What grades did the students in the math class get on their tests?

This question is a statistical question since the expected answers are the different grades students got on the test.

▶ Question 4 is a statistical question because there is variability in the data, the grades that the students in math class got on the test.

TRY Decide which of the following are statistical questions and which are not. Answer *statistical* or *not statistical* to each question.

a. How many years old are the twin boys?

b. How old are the players on the basketball team?

c. How much taller are you this year than last year?

d. How much does the laptop computer you saw last night cost?

e. How many days does it typically snow in March in each state?

EXAMPLE B Students in a science class want to collect data on the amount of physical activity in which their classmates participate each week. What is a statistical question the students can ask to collect the data?

1

Analyze the kind of data the students want to collect.

The students are looking for amounts of physical activity.

Too general: Do you exercise sometimes?

Too specific: Do you exercise 1 hour every day?

Both of these questions have yes/no answers. Answers to these questions do not lend themselves to further analysis. There will be no way to tell how many hours or days the students who were questioned exercised.

2

Design the question.

The students can ask their classmates how many days they exercise each week and for how long. However, this might be too much data to interpret.

A better question might focus on the number of days per week the classmates exercise for a minimal amount of time, such as 30 minutes.

Sample question: How many days each week do you get at least 30 minutes of physical activity?

3

Review the question.

Check that the question has statistical variability. The answers to the sample question can be any of the numbers 0–7, which correspond to the number of days students get at least 30 minutes of physical activity.

▶ An appropriate statistical question that will result in the desired data is the following: How many days each week do you get at least 30 minutes of physical activity?

MODEL

Suppose you wanted to collect data on how much time your classmates spend watching TV. Write a sample question you could ask that would help you obtain the desired data.

Practice

Choose the best answer.

1. Carlotta is taking a survey to determine the ages of students enrolled in an art camp. She has a list of four questions that she can ask. Which of the following questions are statistical and which are nonstatistical?

   A. How old is the oldest student in the camp?

   B. How old is the youngest student in the camp?

   C. How old are the students enrolled in the camp?

   D. Are there more boys or girls in the camp?

    HINT Data generated from statistical questions have variability.

2. Alexander is interested in comparing the heights of students playing basketball in his middle school. He has a list of four questions that he can ask. Which of the following questions are statistical and which are nonstatistical?

   A. Do you play basketball in a local league?

   B. How tall are the students on the team?

   C. How tall is the team captain?

   D. What is the difference in height between the tallest and shortest team members?

   REMEMBER Alexander should be able to draw conclusions from the answers.

Solve.

3. A music teacher is interested in learning about the amount of time his students spend practicing each week. What statistical question can he ask his students in order to collect the data he wants?

   _____

4. A math teacher wants to know about how long her students are spending on their math homework each night. What statistical question can she ask her students that will allow her to collect the data she wants?

_____

5. Write a statistical question that would help you gather data about the number of miles students at your school walk each week.

_____

6. Write both a nonstatistical question and a statistical question you could ask your classmates about the movies they see each week.

_____

7. Write both a nonstatistical question and a statistical question you could ask your classmates about the weights of their pets.

_____

8. CONCLUDE Which of the following questions should result in a better collection of data. Why?

   A. About how many servings of fruits and vegetables do you consume each day?

   B. Which vegetable do you prefer, asparagus or broccoli?

_____

_____

_____

9. WRITE MATH Explain the difference between a statistical question and a question that is not statistical.

_____

_____

_____

Range and Measures of Center

The **range** of a data set is a measure of the spread in the data. It uses a single number to summarize how the data in the set vary. The **mean**, **median**, and **mode** are three measures of center of a data set. Each uses a single number to summarize all the values in the data set.

EXAMPLE A The table below shows the daily ticket sales for a rock concert. What is the range of the data for the daily ticket sales? What are the mean, median, and mode of the data?

Rock Concert Daily Ticket Sales

Monday	Tuesday	Wednesday	Thursday	Friday	Saturday
454	635	454	843	1,951	1,999

1

Find the range of the data.

Order the data numerically:
454; 454; 635; 843; 1,951; 1,999
Subtract the least number from the greatest number.
1,999 − 454 = 1,545

▶ The range of the data for daily ticket sales is 1,545 tickets.

2

Find the mean number of tickets sold daily.

The mean is the sum of the values divided by the number of values.

$$\text{mean} = \frac{\text{sum of the numbers}}{\text{how many numbers}}$$
$$= \frac{454 + 635 + 454 + 843 + 1,951 + 1,999}{6}$$
$$= \frac{6,336}{6} = 1,056$$

▶ The mean number of tickets sold daily is 1,056 tickets.

4

Find the mode.

The mode is the value that occurs most often in the data set. Only two of the days had the same number of ticket sales. The mode for daily ticket sales is 454 tickets.

▶ The mode for daily ticket sales is 454 tickets.

3

Find the median number of tickets sold daily.

The median is the middle value in an ordered set of values.

There is an even number of values, so the median is the mean of the two middle values.

$$\text{median} = \frac{635 + 843}{2} = \frac{1,478}{2} = 739$$

▶ The median number of tickets sold daily is 739.

TRY

Find the range, mean, median, and mode of the following data set.

22, 8, 17, 29, 18, 8

EXAMPLE B The daily student attendance at a middle school for 10 school days is shown below.

259, 242, 250, 247, 256, 204, 194, 186, 180, 252

What are the mean and the median daily attendance for the 10-day period? Which measure appears to describe the data set more accurately?

1

Find the mean daily attendance.

$$\text{mean} = \frac{259 + 242 + 250 + 247 + 256 + 204 + 194 + 186 + 180 + 252}{10}$$

$$= \frac{2,270}{10} = 227$$

The mean daily attendance is 227 students.

2

Find the median daily attendance.

Order the values from least to greatest.

180, 186, 194, 204, <u>242</u>, <u>247</u>, 250, 252, 256, 259

Since there is an even number of values, the median is the mean of the two middle values.

$$\text{median} = \frac{242 + 247}{2} = \frac{489}{2} = 244.5$$

The median daily attendance is 244.5 students.

3

Compare the mean and the median as measures of center.

The mean is less than the median. The mean is affected by the three lowest values. Since 6 of the 10 values are greater than 240, the median appears to be closer to most of the values in the data set.

▶ The mean daily attendance is 227 students, and the median daily attendance is 244.5 students. Since more of the values in the set are greater than the mean, the median appears to describe the set more accurately.

DISCUSS

Suppose the school's funding depends on average daily attendance. Which measure of center would the school administrators prefer to use in reporting the average daily attendance? Explain.

EXAMPLE C Mr. Kell earns a commission on his daily sales. Below are the commissions he earned on sales for a 15-day period. What is the range in his commissions for that period? Does the range seem like a good description of this data set? How does the range compare with the mean or the median as a description of Mr. Kell's commissions for the 15-day period?

$85, $92, $86, $75, $88, $142, $90, $82, $76, $94, $87, $93, $68, $79, $84

1

Find the range.

range = greatest commission − least commission = $142 − $68 = $74

The range in the commissions is $74.

2

Find the mean.

$$\frac{85 + 92 + 86 + 75 + 88 + 142 + 90 + 82 + 76 + 94 + 87 + 93 + 68 + 79 + 84}{15} = \frac{1{,}321}{15} = 88.0\overline{6}$$

The mean is about $88.07.

3

Find the median.

List the numbers in numerical order, and find the middle value.

68, 75, 76, 79, 82, 84, 85, <u>86</u>, 87, 88, 90, 92, 93, 94, 142

The median commission is $86.

4

Decide if the range describes the data well. Compare it with the median and the mean.

▶ The range of $74 means that there was a variation of $74 in his commissions during the 15-day period. This would indicate that there is quite a lot of variability in the commissions Mr. Kell earns. However, the data show that 10 of the 15 commissions were between $80 and $95, which is less variability than the range indicates. The mean is more typical of the commissions, but it is also affected by the **outlier**, 142.

Since 9 of the 15 values are less than the mean, the median is probably the best measure to use in describing this data set.

DISCUSS

Values that are much greater or much less than other values in a data set are called outliers. How would the removal of $68 and $142 from the set of commissions above affect the range, mean, and median?

Problem Solving

READ

The table shows Kevin's scores in four quizzes. What score does he need in the fifth quiz to have a mean score of 92 for all 5 quizzes?

Kevin's Math Quiz Scores

Quiz	Score
1	85
2	94
3	89
4	98
5	?

PLAN

Step 1: Find the total number of points Kevin has in the first four quizzes.

Step 2: Find the total number of points he needs to have a mean score of 92 in 5 quizzes.

Step 3: Find the difference between the total number of points needed and the number of points he already has to find the number of points he needs in the fifth quiz.

SOLVE

Step 1: How many points does Kevin have on the first 4 quizzes?

85 + _____ + _____ + _____ = _____

Step 2: How many points does Kevin need in all?

92 × 5 = _____

Step 3: How many points does Kevin need on quiz 5?

_____ − _____ = _____

CHECK

Add the answer you found in Step 3 to the numbers given in the table above.

85 + 94 + 89 + 98 + _____ = _____

Divide the sum by 5. If the result is a mean score of _____, the answer is correct.

_____ ÷ 5 = _____

▶ Kevin needs a score of _____ to have a mean score of 92 on the 5 quizzes.

Practice

Use the graph for questions 1–4.

The graph shows the number of students from different grades who attended a karate camp.

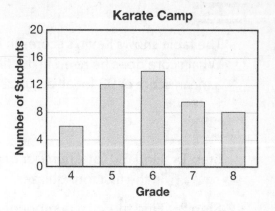

Karate Camp

1. What is the mean number of students that attended the camp? _____

2. What is the median number of students that attended the camp? _____

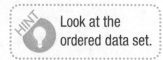

Look at the ordered data set.

3. What is the mode number of students that attended the camp? _____

REMEMBER There can be no mode, one mode, or more than one mode in a data set.

4. What is the range of students per grade that attended the camp? _____

Solve.

5. Rod's scores on 4 history tests are 88, 96, 98, and 90. What score does he need on the fifth test to have a mean score of 94 on all 5 tests? _____

6. The table shows the number of soccer fans in each grade at Jamie's school. What are the mean, median, mode, and range of the data? Which of these is a measure of variation? Which measure of center would you choose as best describing the data in the set? Explain your choice.

Soccer Fans

Grade	Number of Students
3	32
4	41
5	27
6	32
7	39
8	27

_____

_____

7. Students in Ms. Carrey's science class recorded the low temperatures for one week. The graph shows the temperatures they recorded each day. What are the mean, median, mode, and range? Round each value to the nearest degree if necessary. How would you use the points in the graph to find the range?

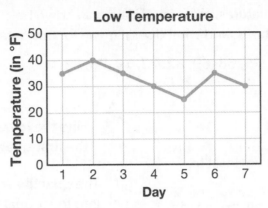

_____

_____

_____

8. ANALYZE How would you use the points on the graph in question 7 to recognize the mode? Explain.

_____

_____

_____

9. WRITE MATH Summarize the steps you would take to find the range and measures of center for a given data set.

_____

_____

_____

34 Measures of Variability

The **interquartile range (IQR)** is a measure of the spread of the middle half of a data set.

EXAMPLE A The high temperatures, in °F, for 11 days are shown below. What is the IQR of the temperatures, and what does it mean for this data?

70, 68, 72, 75, 68, 69, 82, 73, 79, 78, 83

1

Find the median.

List the numbers in order from least to greatest.

68, 68, 69, 70, 72, 73, 75, 78, 79, 82, 83

Find the middle number.

68, 68, 69, 70, 72, _73_, 75, 78, 79, 82, 83

The median is 73.

2

Find the **lower quartile**, also called the **first quartile** or Q1.

The **quartiles** of a data set divide the set into four equal parts.

The median of the data set is the middle quartile.

The median of the lower half of the data set is the lower quartile.

List the values in the lower half of the data in order from least to greatest. Then find the median of the lower half of the data.

68, 68, _69_, 70, 72

The lower quartile is 69.

3

Find the **upper quartile**, also called the **third quartile** or Q3.

The median of the upper half of the data is the upper quartile.

List the values in the upper half of the data in order from least to greatest. Then find the median of the upper half of the data.

75, 78, _79_, 82, 83

The upper quartile is 79.

4

Find the IQR.

The IQR is the difference between the upper quartile and the lower quartile.

IQR = 79 − 69 = 10

So there is a 10°F spread in the middle half of the data.

▶ The IQR is 10°F. An IQR of 10°F means that there is a 10°F spread in the high temperatures in the middle half of the data (the data between the upper and lower quartiles).

DISCUSS

How does the variability in the spread of the IQR of the temperatures compare with the variability in the spread of the range of the temperatures?

The **mean absolute deviation** measures the average amount that the items of a data set differ from the mean of the set.

EXAMPLE B Otto's test scores on five science tests are 87, 79, 82, 89, and 93. What is the mean absolute deviation of his test scores, and what does it indicate for this data?

1

Find the mean of Otto's test scores.

$$\text{mean} = \frac{87 + 79 + 82 + 89 + 93}{5} = \frac{430}{5} = 86$$

2

Find the difference of each score from the mean score.

Subtract the lesser value from the greater value, so each difference is positive.

$87 - 86 = 1$

$86 - 79 = 7$

$86 - 82 = 4$

$89 - 86 = 3$

$93 - 86 = 7$

3

Find the mean absolute deviation.

mean absolute deviation
$$= \frac{1 + 7 + 4 + 3 + 7}{5} = \frac{22}{5}$$
$$= 4\frac{2}{5} \text{ or } 4.4$$

The mean absolute deviation is 4.4. It indicates that the average difference of Otto's test scores from the mean is 4.4 points.

▶ The mean absolute deviation is 4.4. It indicates that the average difference of Otto's test scores from the mean score of 86 is 4.4 points.

TRY

Find the mean absolute deviation for the following data set.

93, 87, 84, 91, 85

Practice

Use Zahra's bowling scores for questions 1–9.

Zahra's bowling scores: 124, 150, 138, 172

1. What is Zahra's mean score? What is her median score? _____

2. How do the mean and median compare as measures of center?

_____

3. What is the range in Zahra's bowling scores? _____

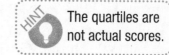

The quartiles are not actual scores.

4. Find the lower and upper quartiles of her scores. _____

5. What is the interquartile range of the scores? _____

6. How do the range and the interquartile range compare as measures of the variability of the scores?

_____

7. What is the difference of each score from the mean? _____

REMEMBER Subtract so that the differences are all positive.

8. What is the mean absolute deviation of the bowling scores? _____

9. Interpret the mean absolute deviation of the scores.

_____

Use the dog weights for questions 10–12.

The dogs' weights, in pounds, recorded one day at a vet's office:

71, 34, 15, 23, 18, 56, 63

10. What is the mean weight? What is the median weight? How do the mean and median compare as measures of center?

_____

11. What is the range of the weights? What is the interquartile range? How do the range and the interquartile range compare as measures of the variability of the scores?

_____

12. What is the mean absolute deviation of the weights? Interpret the mean absolute deviation of the dogs' weights.

_____

Use the following information for questions 13–15.

Sagar planted some sunflowers in his garden. The sunflowers grew to the following heights, in centimeters:

200, 204, 198, 172, 196

13. How does the mean height compare with the median height of the sunflowers?

_____

14. How does the interquartile range compare with the range of the heights?

_____

15. What is the mean absolute deviation? What does this indicate about the heights of the sunflowers?

_____

Solve.

16. Attendance at the science fair for the last eight years was 86, 72, 98, 106, 112, 65, 102, and 96. What is the range in the attendance? What is the interquartile range? What do they indicate about the variability in the spread of the attendance?

_____

_____

_____

17. DIFFERENTIATE Distinguish between the way in which a measure of center describes a data set and the way in which a measure of variability describes a data set.

_____

_____

_____

35 Displaying Data Using Dot Plots

EXAMPLE A Students held a car wash to raise money for charity. The **dot plot** shows the amount of money they collected for each vehicle they washed. How many vehicles did they wash? What is the mean amount they collected per vehicle? What is the median amount collected per vehicle?

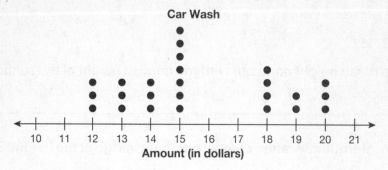

Car Wash

Amount (in dollars)

1

Find the total number of vehicles washed.

Count the number of dots. There are 25 dots, or observations. Each dot represents a single observation, the amount that students collected for one car wash, in dollars.

▶ So the students washed 25 vehicles at their car wash.

2

Find the mean.

Multiply each amount by the number of observations, or dots: 3 × 12 = 36, 3 × 13 = 39, 3 × 14 = 42, 7 × 15 = 105, 4 × 18 = 72, 2 × 19 = 38, 3 × 20 = 60

Find the sum of the products: 36 + 39 + 42 + 105 + 72 + 38 + 60 = 392

Divide by the number of observations: 392 ÷ 25 = 15.68

▶ So the mean is $15.68.

3

Find the median.

The median is the middle point in 25 points. It is the 13th point in order from the beginning of the data set (or from the end). Count the points up to the 13th point.

▶ The 13th point occurs at $15. So the median is $15.

DISCUSS

What is the mode of the amounts students collected? How do you know?

EXAMPLE B Nevena surveyed 20 students to find the number of calls they made in a 24-hour period. Her results are shown below. Make a dot plot of the data. Are there any patterns or deviations in the data?

4, 3, 4, 5, 0, 2, 4, 4, 5, 9, 4, 5, 4, 1, 0, 5, 3, 3, 5, 6

1 Find the minimum and maximum values.

The least value is 0, and the greatest value is 9.

2 Draw the dot plot.

Draw a number line from 0 to 10.

Draw a dot above the number line to show each observation in the list.

Label the number line to show the units.

Give the dot plot a title.

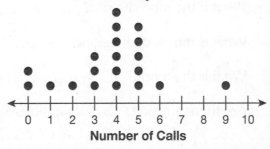

Calls Made by Students

3 Look for patterns or deviations in the data.

The dot plot provides a picture of the data.

There is a cluster of points from 3 to 5.

There is an outlier at 9.

The dot plot shows that most students made between 3 and 5 calls.

▶ The dot plot is shown on the right. The dots cluster at points 3 to 5, which indicates that most students made between 3 and 5 calls. There is an outlier at 9, which means that 9 calls was a significantly greater number of calls than were made by most students.

DISCUSS

Find the mean and the median number of calls. Are the results surprising? Explain why or why not.

Practice

Use the dot plot for questions 1–8.

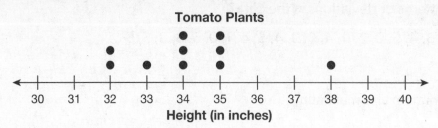

Tomato Plants

Height (in inches)

1. How many tomato plants were observed? _____

2. What does the dot plot show? _____

3. What units were used to make the measurements? _____

4. Find the range in the heights. _____

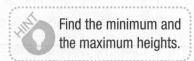
HINT — Find the minimum and the maximum heights.

5. What is the mean height? _____

6. What is the median height? _____

7. What is the mode? _____

REMEMBER The mode may not be unique.

8. Are there any patterns or deviations in the data? Explain.

_____

Use the data for questions 9–10.

The number of books read by students over break:

6, 5, 6, 10, 8, 10, 5, 10, 6, 5, 5, 7, 10, 7, 10

9. Make a dot plot to show the data.

10. Are there any patterns or deviations in the data? Explain.

_____

Use the information and dot plot for questions 11–14.

The dot plot shows the results
of a one-kilometer fun run.

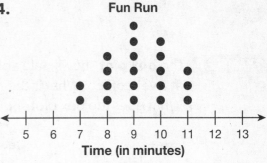

Fun Run

Time (in minutes)

11. What does each dot represent?

_____

12. Compare the mean, median, and mode of the times.

_____

13. What does the range tell about the variability in the times?

_____

14. Are there any patterns or deviations in the data? Explain.

_____

Solve.

15. **EXAMINE** Compare the usefulness of a dot plot with that of a bar or line graph with respect to determining the median of a data set.

_____

_____

16. **DEMONSTRATE** Students did push-ups for a fitness test. The results are shown below.

25, 25, 23, 30, 24, 24, 25, 24, 23, 24, 20, 24, 25, 23, 25

Use the results to make a dot plot of the data. Are there any patterns or deviations in the data? Explain.

_____

_____

36 Displaying Data Using Box Plots

EXAMPLE A The **box plot** shows data about the weights of cats that were treated one day at a vet's office. What is the range in the weights? What is the interquartile range? What does the box plot show about the variability in the cats' weights?

Cat Weights (in pounds)

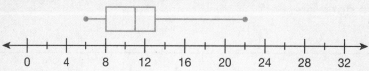

1

Identify the measures that the box plot reports.

The box plot provides a summary of the data. It does not preserve the actual data, so it does not show the number of observations. It provides a picture of a five-number summary of the data.

The measures shown in the box plot are the following:

> minimum: 6 lb
> lower quartile: 8 lb
> median: 11 lb
> upper quartile: 13 lb
> maximum: 22 lb

2

Find the range and the interquartile range.

range = maximum value − minimum value = 22 − 6 = 16

interquartile range = upper quartile − lower quartile = 13 − 8 = 5

The range is 16 lb and the interquartile range is 5 lb.

3

Analyze the variability.

The middle half of the data lies between 8 and 13. So the middle half of the cats that were treated weighed between 8 and 13 pounds. There is more variability in the upper half of data (from median to maximum) than in the lower half of data (from minimum to median). So the range of weights for the cats weighing from 11 to 22 pounds was greater than the range of weights for the cats weighing from 6 to 11 pounds. There is also more variability in the upper quarter of the data than in the lower 75% of the data. So the range of weights for the cats weighing from 13 to 22 pounds was greater than the range of weights for the cats weighing from 6 to 13 pounds.

▶ There is not much variability in the weights between 6 and 13 pounds. Most the variability was in the weights between 13 and 22 pounds.

DISCUSS

Why can't you find the mean or the mode of the data from a box plot?

EXAMPLE B The test scores of 15 students are shown below. Make a box plot of the data. Use your box plot to describe the spread of the data.

80, 85, 75, 80, 85, 90, 90, 95, 85, 85, 80, 80, 85, 80, 90

1

Find the median.

Write the test scores in order from least to greatest.

75, 80, 80, 80, 80, 80, 85, <u>85</u>, 85, 85, 85, 90, 90, 90, 95

The median test score is 85.

2

Find the quartiles, and identify the minimum and maximum.

The lower quartile is the median of the lower half of the data.

75, 80, 80, **80**, 80, 80, 85, <u>85</u>, 85, 85, 85, 90, 90, 90, 95

The upper quartile is the median of the upper half of the data.

75, 80, 80, 80, 80, 80, 85, <u>85</u>, 85, 85, 85, **90**, 90, 90, 95

The lower quartile is 80, and the upper quartile is 90.

The minimum is 75, and the maximum is 95.

3

Draw the box plot.

Draw a number line from 70 to 100 with tick marks at every 5 points. Above the number line, draw the box. Use the lower quartile as the left edge, the median as the vertical line inside the box, and the upper quartile as the right edge. Draw points at the minimum value and the maximum value. Make the "whiskers" by drawing a line to connect the minimum to Q1 and another line to connect the maximum to Q3. Give the box plot a title.

Test Scores

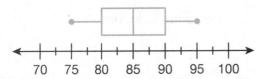

4

Describe the spread of the data.

The box plot shows that the scores are very evenly distributed. The middle half of the scores range from 80 to 90. The bottom quarter of the scores are 75. The top quarter of the scores are 95.

▶ The box plot is shown above. It shows that the test scores are evenly distributed. The median score is 85. The middle half of the scores range from 80 to 90, the minimum score is 75, and the maximum score is 95.

DISCUSS

Explain how you know from the shape of the box plot that the test scores are evenly distributed.

Practice

Use the box plot for questions 1–8.

Volunteer Ages

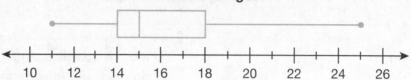

1. What is the range? _____

2. What is the median? _____

3. What is the interquartile range? _____

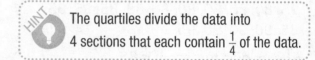

HINT The quartiles divide the data into 4 sections that each contain $\frac{1}{4}$ of the data.

4. What percent of the volunteers were between 14 and 15 years old? _____

5. What percent of the volunteers were between 15 and 18 years old? _____

6. Is there more variability in the lower half of the data or the upper half of the data? How do you know?

_____

7. Are there any extreme values? Explain.

_____

REMEMBER The ends of the "whiskers" are actual values.

8. What does the box plot show about the variability of the ages?

_____

Use the data for questions 9 and 10.

The following are the heights of students on a recreation soccer team, in inches:

58, 53, 59, 58, 60, 57, 62, 55, 57, 56, 58, 59, 56

9. Make a box plot to show the data.

10. What does the box plot show about the variability of the heights?

_____

Use the information and the box plot for questions 11–13.

The box plot shows the points scored during the season for Vickie's team.

Game Scores

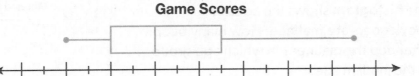

11. What does the range tell about the variability in the scores?

_____

12. What does the interquartile range tell about the variability in the scores?

_____

13. What does the box plot show about the variability of the scores?

_____

_____

Solve.

14. CONCLUDE What is the five-number summary of a data set? How is it used to make a box plot?

_____

_____

_____

15. CONSTRUCT The ages of the first 15 presidents at their first inaugurations are shown below.

57, 61, 57, 57, 57, 58, 57, 61, 54, 68, 51, 49, 64, 50, 48

Make a box plot of the data. What does the box plot show about the variability of the ages?

_____

_____

_____

37 Displaying Data Using Histograms

EXAMPLE A The **histogram** shows the ages of moviegoers at a matinee. How many people attended the matinee? In which age group is the median age?

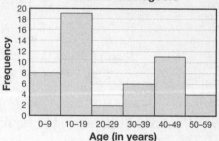

Matinee Moviegoers

Understand how to read a histogram.

The vertical axis on a histogram represents the frequency, which means the number of observations. For this histogram, the frequency represents the number of people who attended the matinee. Each interval along the horizontal axis represents a span of ages.

The heights of the bars show the number of people in each age group.

② Find the number of people who attended the matinee.

Use the graph to make a frequency table.

Age Interval	Frequency
0–9	8
10–19	19
20–29	2
30–39	6
40–49	11
50–59	4

Find the sum of the frequencies.

$8 + 19 + 2 + 6 + 11 + 4 = 50$

So 50 people attended the matinee.

Find the age group in which the median lies.

The median is the middle number in an ordered set of data.

The intervals are ordered from least to greatest. There are 50 people.

Since 50 is an even number, the median is between the 25th and 26th frequencies.

Since $8 + 19 = 27$, the median occurs in the second interval, which contains the ages 10–19.

▶ 50 people attended the matinee. The median is in the 10–19 year age interval.

Can you find the exact mean, median, or mode from a histogram? Explain why or why not.

EXAMPLE B The frequency table shows the length of time in minutes that sixth-grade students at a middle school played video games on a school holiday. Make a histogram of the data. What does the shape of the histogram show about the lengths of times the students played video games that day?

Time in Minutes	Frequency
0–29	30
30–59	45
60–89	25
90–119	10
120–149	15

1

Choose an interval for the vertical axis.

The frequencies vary from 10 to 45.

Use an interval of 10 from 0 to 50.

2

Make the histogram.

The vertical axis shows the frequency. Label the axis. The horizontal axis is divided into equal intervals. Label each interval. There is no space between intervals except for those that contain no data. Draw bars that show the frequencies from the table. Shade each bar differently. Give the histogram a title.

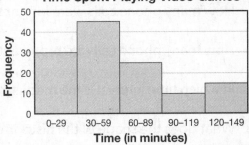

3

Examine the shape of the histogram.

Most students played video games for 30–59 minutes.

▶ The histogram is shown on the right. The lengths of time cluster from 0–89 minutes and then drop off.

DISCUSS

Can you determine the exact range in a histogram? Explain why or why not.

Practice

Use the histogram for questions 1–6.

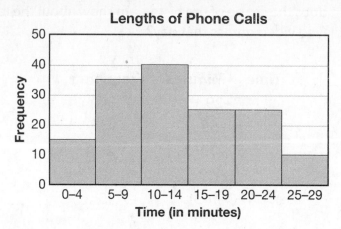

Lengths of Phone Calls

1. Which time interval had the greatest number of phone calls? _____

    Find the tallest bar.

2. How many phone calls were less than 15 minutes long? _____

   REMEMBER Find the frequency of all the intervals less than 15.

3. How many phone calls were longer than 19 minutes? _____

4. How many phone calls are represented in all? _____

5. In which time interval is the median? _____

6. What does the shape of the histogram show about the length of the phone calls?

   _____

   _____

Use the data for questions 7 and 8.

Each student in the sixth-grade English classes
in Richard's school told the number of pages
in the last book he or she read. The English teacher
summarized the data in the frequency
table shown.

Number of Pages	Frequency
0–49	6
50–99	12
100–149	10
150–199	18
200–249	4

7. Make a histogram of the data.

8. What does the shape of the histogram show about the number of pages in the last book
each student read?

_____

Solve.

9. ANALYZE On a bar graph, the tallest or longest bar represents the mode. However, on a
histogram, the mode may not lie in the interval with the tallest bar. Explain why.

_____

_____

10. DECIDE Students recorded the number of minutes they spent working on a science
project. The times are shown below.

35, 48, 26, 18, 85, 74, 65, 38, 42, 73, 65, 55

What interval lengths would you use to make a histogram of the data? Explain your choice.

_____

_____

Choosing Measures to Fit Distributions

EXAMPLE A The line plot shows the amount of money Dorian spent on eating lunch out last month. Which measure of center, the mean or the median, better describes the typical or average amount Dorian spent on these lunches? Explain.

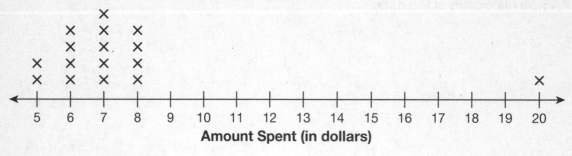

Lunch

Amount Spent (in dollars)

1

Look at the shape of the data.

Most of the data is clustered at the left end, from $5 to $8.

There is one extreme amount at $20.

The $20 amount is an outlier.

2

Decide how the outlier affects the mean and the median.

The mean is affected by outliers.

An outlier can raise or lower the mean.

The median is not affected by an outlier.

An outlier does not raise or lower the median.

3

Decide which measure better describes the amount Dorian spent on lunch.

The median is not affected by the outlier, so the median better describes the data.

▶ The median better describes the average amount Dorian spent eating lunch out last month.

DISCUSS

Why is the mean the only measure of center that is significantly affected by an outlier that is much greater than the other values in a data set?

EXAMPLE B The line plot shows the distances Betsy ran when training for a long-distance race. Which measure, the range or the interquartile range, better describes the variability in the number of miles Betsy ran? Explain.

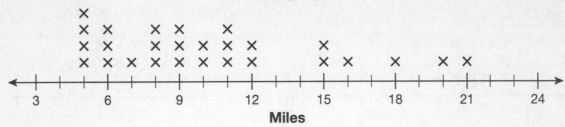

Training Runs

Miles

1

Look at the spread of the data.

Most of the data is between 5 miles and 12 miles.

There are some training runs greater than 12 miles, but there are many more training runs that are less than 12 miles.

2

Analyze the spread of the data.

The range shows the spread of the data from the least value to the greatest value. The range is spread out and shows quite a bit of variation, from 5 miles to 21 miles.

The interquartile range describes the spread of the middle half of the data, which includes training runs from 6 miles to 12 miles. The upper bound of the interquartile range is the upper quartile. Since 75% of the training runs are 12 miles or less, the interquartile range is a better description of the variability of this data set than is the range of the set.

▶ The interquartile range better describes the variability in the number of miles in Betsy's training runs than the range.

CHECK

Find the range and the interquartile range of Betsy's training runs. Do the values support the solution above?

Practice

Use the line plot for questions 1–3.

The line plot shows the weights of packages shipped at a shipping center during one hour.

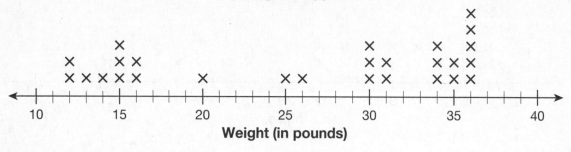

1. Describe the shape of the data.

   _____

2. Which describes the data better, the mean or the median? Explain.

   _____

3. Which describes the variability in the data better, the range or the interquartile range? Explain.

   _____

Use the line plot for questions 4 and 5.

The line plot shows the heights of fruit trees in an orchard.

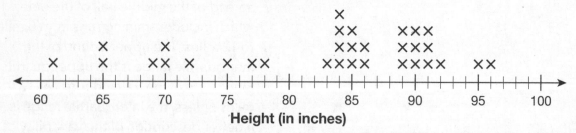

4. Which describes the data better, the mean or the median? Explain.

   _____

5. Which describes the variability better, the range or the interquartile range? Explain.

   _____

Solve.

6. The line plot shows the ages of actors in a community theater play.

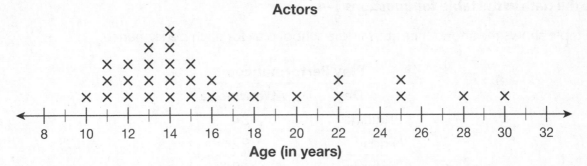

Which measure of center best describes the data? Which measure of variability best describes the data? Use the shape of the data distribution to decide. Explain.

_____

_____

7. The line plot shows the low temperature for 30 days.

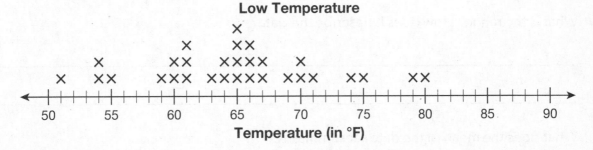

Which measure of center best describes the data? Which measure of variability best describes the data? Use the shape of the data distribution to decide. Explain.

_____

_____

8. **SUMMARIZE** Explain how the shape of the data distribution as shown in a line plot can help you decide which measure of center and which measure of variability best describe the data.

_____

_____

Use the data in the table for questions 1–4.

The table shows the attendance at a middle school play for each performance.

Play Performances

Day	Attendance
Thursday	84
Friday	92
Saturday	148
Sunday	79
Monday	62

1. Find the mean and the median. How do these measures describe the data?

_____

_____

2. What is the range? How does it describe the data?

_____

_____

3. What does the mean of the data set summarize?

_____

4. What does the range of the data set summarize?

_____

Solve.

5. Andrew is taking a survey to determine the ages of students who visited the planetarium. Identify which questions are statistical by writing *statistical* or *not statistical* next to each.

   a. How old are the boys who visited the planetarium? _____

   b. Did more girls or more boys visit the planetarium? _____

6. Lakshmi surveyed 18 classmates to find out how many text messages they sent in one hour. The results are shown below. Use the results to make a dot plot of the data.

5, 4, 5, 14, 28, 15, 16, 14, 5, 7, 5, 4, 2, 10, 15, 1, 4, 6

7. A coach is interested in learning about the amount of time players on the team spend practicing each week during the off-season. What is a statistical question she can ask the players that will help her collect this data?

_____

Use the dot plot for questions 8–13.

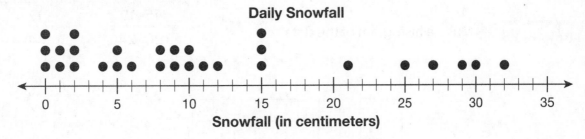

Daily Snowfall

Snowfall (in centimeters)

8. How many days of snowfall does the dot plot represent? _____

9. What does each dot represent?

_____

10. What is the median? _____

11. What is the interquartile range? _____

12. Which would describe the center of the data better, the mean or the median? Explain.

_____

13. Which would describe the variability of the data better, the range or the interquartile range? Explain.

_____

Solve.

14. Draco's test scores on five social studies tests are 86, 93, 92, 80, and 94. What is his mean test score? What is the mean absolute deviation of his test scores? What does the mean absolute deviation of his test scores measure?

_____

_____

Use the data in the table for questions 15–17.

A botanist recorded the heights of different tomato plants after one month. The heights are summarized by the data in the frequency table shown.

Height, centimeters	Frequency
0–4	6
5–9	8
10–14	15
15–19	17
20–24	4

15. How many tomato plants did the botanist measure? _____

16. DEMONSTRATE Make a histogram of the data.

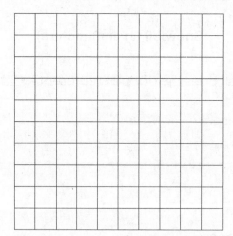

17. CONCLUDE What is the overall pattern of the heights shown in the histogram?

_____

_____

Information Please

Work alone, with a partner, or with a small group of your classmates.

1. Choose a statistical question to use in a survey. You can use one of the following suggestions or make up your own question.

> How many books have you read in the past six months?
>
> How many minutes do you spend traveling to and from school each day?

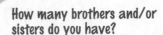

> How many brothers and/or sisters do you have?
>
> How many hours a week do you watch TV?

Your question should result in answers that can be compiled in a dot plot, a box plot, and a histogram.

2. Survey 20 people in your school, in your class, among your friends, or in your family. Record the results in a frequency table.

3. Find the range, mean, median, and mode of the data.

4. Give a five-number summary of the data: the minimum, the lower quartile, the median, the upper quartile, and the maximum.

5. Find the interquartile range.

6. Make a dot plot of the data.

7. Make a box plot of the data.

8. Make a histogram of the data.

9. Analyze the data.

   Do the graphs show any patterns or deviations?

   Which measures of center and variability best describe your data?

   Write a paragraph summarizing your results. In your discussion of the results, be sure to talk about what the measures and patterns mean in relation to the survey question.

Glossary

absolute value the distance of a number from zero on a number line (Lesson 14)

algebraic expression a mathematical statement that combines numbers, operation signs, and variables (Lesson 20)

area a measure of the number of square units needed to cover a region (Lesson 27)

base (of a figure) the bottom face of a three-dimensional figure; the bottom and top faces of a three-dimensional figure (Lesson 30)

base (of an expression) the repeated factor in an expression with an exponent (Lesson 19)

box plot a graph that shows the least and greatest values, lower (first) and upper (third) quartiles, and median of a data set (Lesson 36)

capacity the amount that a container can hold (Lesson 6)

coefficient the numerical factor of a term containing a variable (Lesson 20)

compatible numbers numbers that are close in value to the exact numbers and that are easy to use when computing (Lesson 9)

coordinate plane a plane formed by the intersection of a horizontal number line, the x-axis, and a vertical number line, the y-axis (Lessons 3, 17)

customary system the system of measurement used in the United States (Lesson 6)

dependent variable in an equation with two variables, the variable whose value is affected by the independent variable; in $y = x + 1$, y is the dependent variable (Lesson 25)

distributive property a property that states that multiplying the sum of two numbers by another number gives the same result as multiplying each addend by the number and then adding the products; the property also applies to subtraction (Lesson 12)

dividend a number to be divided (Lesson 7)

divisor the number by which the dividend is divided (Lesson 7)

dot plot a data display in which each data item is shown as a dot above a number line (Lesson 35)

equation a statement that two quantities are equal; contains an equal sign ($=$) (Lesson 23)

equivalent ratios ratios $\frac{a}{b}$ and $\frac{c}{d}$ are equivalent if $ad = bc$, where $b \neq 0$ and $d \neq 0$ (Lesson 3)

exponent a number that tells how many times a given number is used as a factor (Lesson 19)

expression a phrase that contains numbers and operations (Lesson 19)

face a flat surface of a solid figure (Lesson 30)

factor a number that divides evenly into a given number (Lesson 12)

first quartile the median of the lower half of the data in a data set; sometimes called the lower quartile or Q1 (Lesson 34)

greatest common factor (GCF) the greatest factor that is common to two or more numbers (Lessons 12, 22)

histogram a bar graph that shows the frequency of data within equal intervals (Lesson 37)

independent variable in an equation with two variables, the variable whose value affects the dependent variable; in $y = x + 1$, x is the independent variable (Lesson 25)

inequality a mathematical statement that compares two expressions and includes an inequality symbol such as $<$, $>$, $\leq$, or $\geq$ (Lesson 24)

integers the set of counting numbers $(1, 2, 3, \ldots)$, their opposites $(-1, -2, -3, \ldots)$, and zero (Lesson 13)

interquartile range (IQR) the difference between the upper (third) and lower (first) quartiles in a data set (Lesson 34)

inverse operations operations that undo each other, such as addition and subtraction or multiplication and division (Lesson 23)

least common multiple (LCM) the least number that is a multiple of two or more numbers (Lesson 12)

lower quartile the median of the lower half of the data in a data set; sometimes called the first quartile or Q1 (Lesson 34)

mass the amount of matter in an object (Lesson 6)

mean the sum of the values in a data set divided by the number of values in the data set (Lesson 33)

mean absolute deviation a measure of the amount of variability in a data set; the mean of the absolute values of the deviations from the mean in a data set (Lesson 34)

median the middle value in a data set ordered from least to greatest or from greatest to least (Lesson 33)

metric system a system of measurement used in most parts of the world other than the United States; it is based on powers of 10 (Lesson 6)

mode the value or values that occur most often in a data set (Lesson 33)

multiple a product of two numbers (Lesson 12)

negative numbers any number less than zero; located to the left of 0 on a number line (Lesson 13)

net a flat pattern that can be folded into a three-dimensional figure; it shows each surface of the solid figure it forms (Lesson 30)

numerical expression a combination of numbers and operation signs (Lesson 19)

opposites two numbers represented by points on the number line that are the same distance from zero and on opposite sides of zero (Lesson 13)

order of operations a set of rules that determines the correct sequence for evaluating expressions (Lesson 19)

ordered pair a pair of numbers in the form (x, y) that gives the location of a point on a coordinate plane (Lessons 3, 17)

origin the point on a coordinate plane where the x-axis and the y-axis intersect, located at $(0, 0)$ (Lessons 3, 17)

outlier a value in a data set that is much less or much greater than the other values in the set (Lesson 33)

parallelogram a quadrilateral with 2 pairs of opposite sides that are parallel and with opposite sides the same length (Lesson 27)

percent (%) a ratio that compares a number to 100; "per 100" or "out of 100" (Lesson 5)

positive numbers any numbers greater than zero; located to the right of 0 on a number line (Lesson 13)

pyramid a three-dimensional figure with a polygon base and all other faces are triangles that meet at a common vertex (Lesson 30)

quadrant any of the four sections of a coordinate plane separated by the x-axis and y-axis (Lesson 17)

quadrilateral a polygon with 4 sides and 4 angles (Lesson 27)

quartile one of the three values that divide the data set into four quarters (Lesson 34)

quotient the answer to a division problem (Lesson 7)

range the difference of the least value and the greatest value in a data set (Lesson 33)

rate a ratio that compares two quantities with different units of measure (Lesson 2)

ratio a comparison of two numbers (Lesson 1)

rational number a number that can be expressed as the ratio of two integers in the form $\frac{a}{b}$, where b is not equal to 0 (Lesson 15)

reciprocals number pairs that have a product of 1 (Lesson 7)

rectangular prism a three-dimensional figure with six rectangular faces (Lesson 28)

rectangular pyramid a solid figure with 4 triangular faces and a rectangular base (Lesson 30)

remainder a number that is left after division has been completed (Lesson 9)

right triangle a triangle with one right angle (Lesson 27)

surface area the total area of the surfaces of a solid figure (Lesson 31)

term a number, variable, product, or quotient in an expression (Lesson 20)

third quartile the median of the upper half of the data in a data set; sometimes called the upper quartile or Q3 (Lesson 34)

three-dimensional figure a figure that has length, width, and height (Lesson 30)

trapezoid a quadrilateral with exactly 1 pair of parallel sides (Lesson 27)

triangle a polygon with 3 sides and 3 angles (Lesson 27)

triangular prism a three-dimensional figure with 2 triangular faces and 3 rectangular faces (Lesson 30)

two-dimensional figure a flat shape that has length and width (Lesson 30)

unit rate a rate in which the second measurement or amount is 1 unit (Lessons 2, 4)

upper quartile the median of the upper half of the data in a data set; sometimes called the third quartile or Q3 (Lesson 34)

variable a letter or symbol used to represent a number (Lesson 20)

volume the number of cubic units needed to fill a three-dimensional figure (Lesson 28)

x-axis the horizontal axis on a coordinate plane (Lessons 3, 17)

x-coordinate the first number in an ordered pair (Lesson 3)

y-axis the vertical axis on a coordinate plane (Lessons 3, 17)

y-coordinate the second number in an ordered pair (Lesson 3)

Math Tool: Tables of Measurement Units

Customary Units of Length

1 foot (ft) = 12 inches (in.)

1 yard (yd) = 3 ft

1 yd = 36 in.

1 mile (mi) = 5,280 ft

1 mi = 1,760 yd

Customary Units of Weight

1 pound (lb) = 16 ounces (oz)

1 ton (T) = 2,000 lb

Customary Units of Capacity

1 cup (c) = 8 fluid ounces (oz)

1 pint (pt) = 2 c

1 quart (qt) = 2 pt

1 gallon (gal) = 4 qt

Metric Units of Length

1 centimeter (cm) = 10 millimeters (mm)

1 meter (m) = 100 cm

1 m = 1,000 mm

1 kilometer (km) = 1,000 m

Metric Units of Mass

1 gram (g) = 1,000 milligrams (mg)

1 kilogram (kg) = 1,000 g

1 metric ton (t) = 1,000 kg

Metric Units of Capacity

1 liter (L) = 1,000 milliliters (mL)

1 kiloliter (kL) = 1,000 L

Time

1 minute (min) = 60 seconds (sec)

1 hour (h) = 60 min

1 day (d) = 24 h

1 week (wk) = 7 d

1 year (yr) = 12 months (mo)

1 yr = 52 weeks

1 yr = $365\frac{1}{4}$ d

Square Measure

1 square foot (sq ft or ft^2) = 144 square inches (sq in. or $in.^2$)

1 square yard (sq yd or yd^2) = 9 sq ft

Math Tool: Coordinate Plane

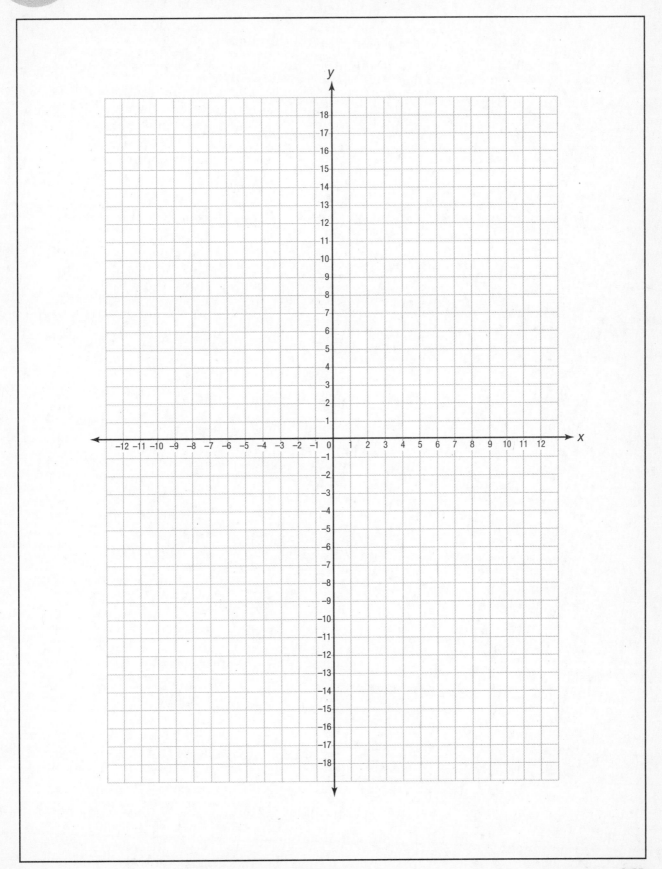

Math Tool: Coordinate Planes

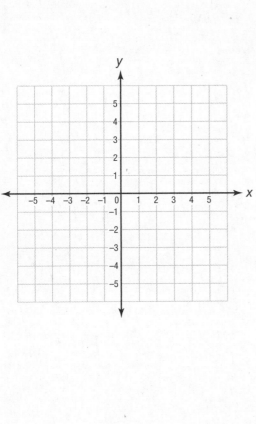

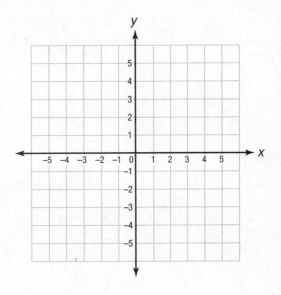

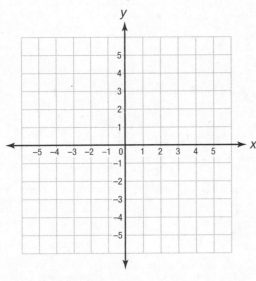

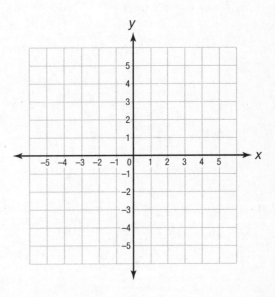

Math Tool: Grids

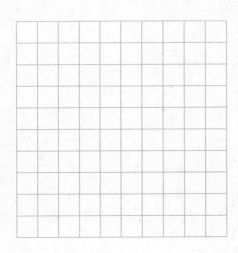

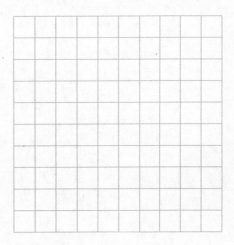

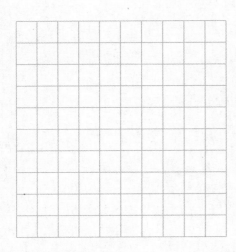

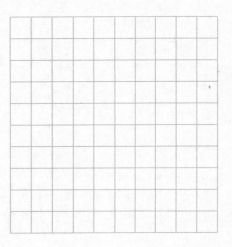

Math Tool: Blank Number Lines

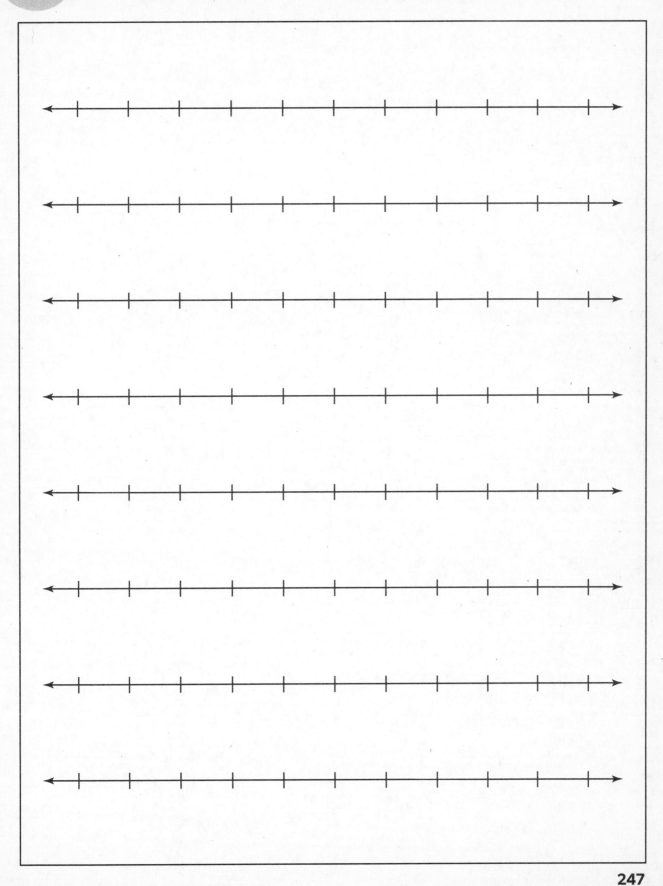

Math Tool: Grid Paper

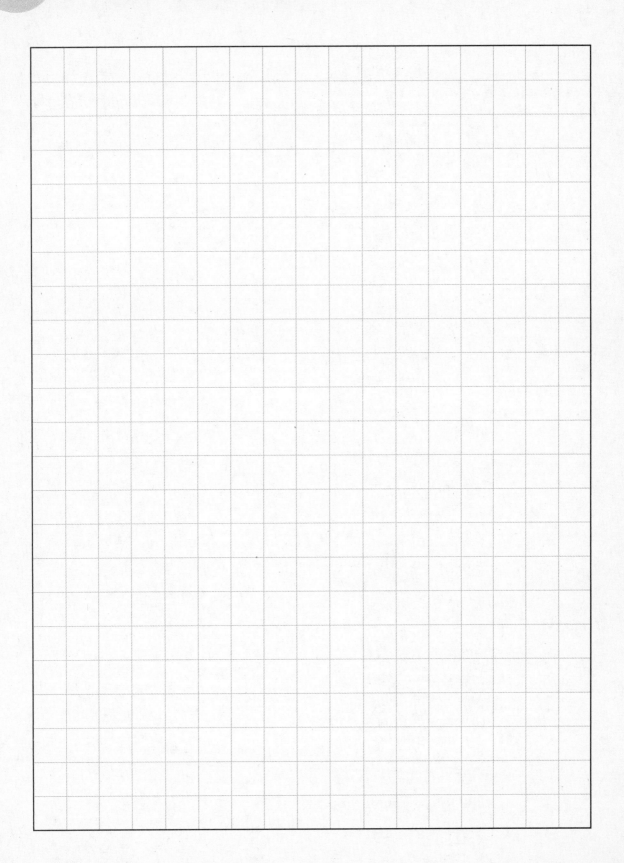

Math Tool: Grid Paper

Math Tool: Area Formulas

Formulas for Area, A	
Rectangle 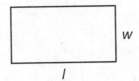 $A = lw,$ where l stands for the length and w stands for the width	**Square** $A = s^2,$ where s stands for the length of a side
Triangle 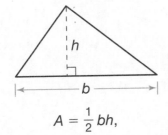 $A = \frac{1}{2}bh,$ where b stands for the length of the base and h stands for the height	**Parallelogram** 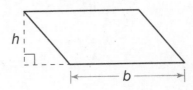 $A = bh,$ where b stands for the length of the base and h stands for the height

Math Tool: Volume Formulas

Formulas for Volume, V

Volume of a Rectangular Prism

$$V = Bh,$$

where B is the area of the base of the prism
and h is the height of the prism

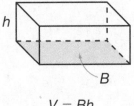

$$V = Bh$$

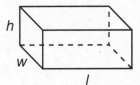

$$V = lwh,$$

where l is the length,
w is the width, and
h is the height

Notes